THERE IS NO
"GOD-GIVEN RIGHT"
TO WORSHIP FALSE GODS

THERE IS NO "GOD-GIVEN RIGHT" TO WORSHIP FALSE GODS

Published by:
R3VOLUTION PRESS
Chapel Hill, TN

Jacket and interior designs by Scott Alan Buss

All Bible verses, unless otherwise noted, are taken from the *English Standard Version* (Copyright © 2001 and used by permission of Crossway Bibles, a division of Good News Publishers).

R3VOLUTION PRESS Books are available at special discounts for bulk purchases. R3VOLUTION PRESS also publishes books in electronic formats. For more information, please visit www.R3VOLUTIONPRESS.com or www.FireBreathingChristian.com.

ISBN 13 Digit: 978-1517766061

Printed in the United States of America

THERE IS NO
"GOD-GIVEN RIGHT"
TO WORSHIP FALSE GODS

(REPENT ACCORDINGLY)

SCOTT ALAN BUSS

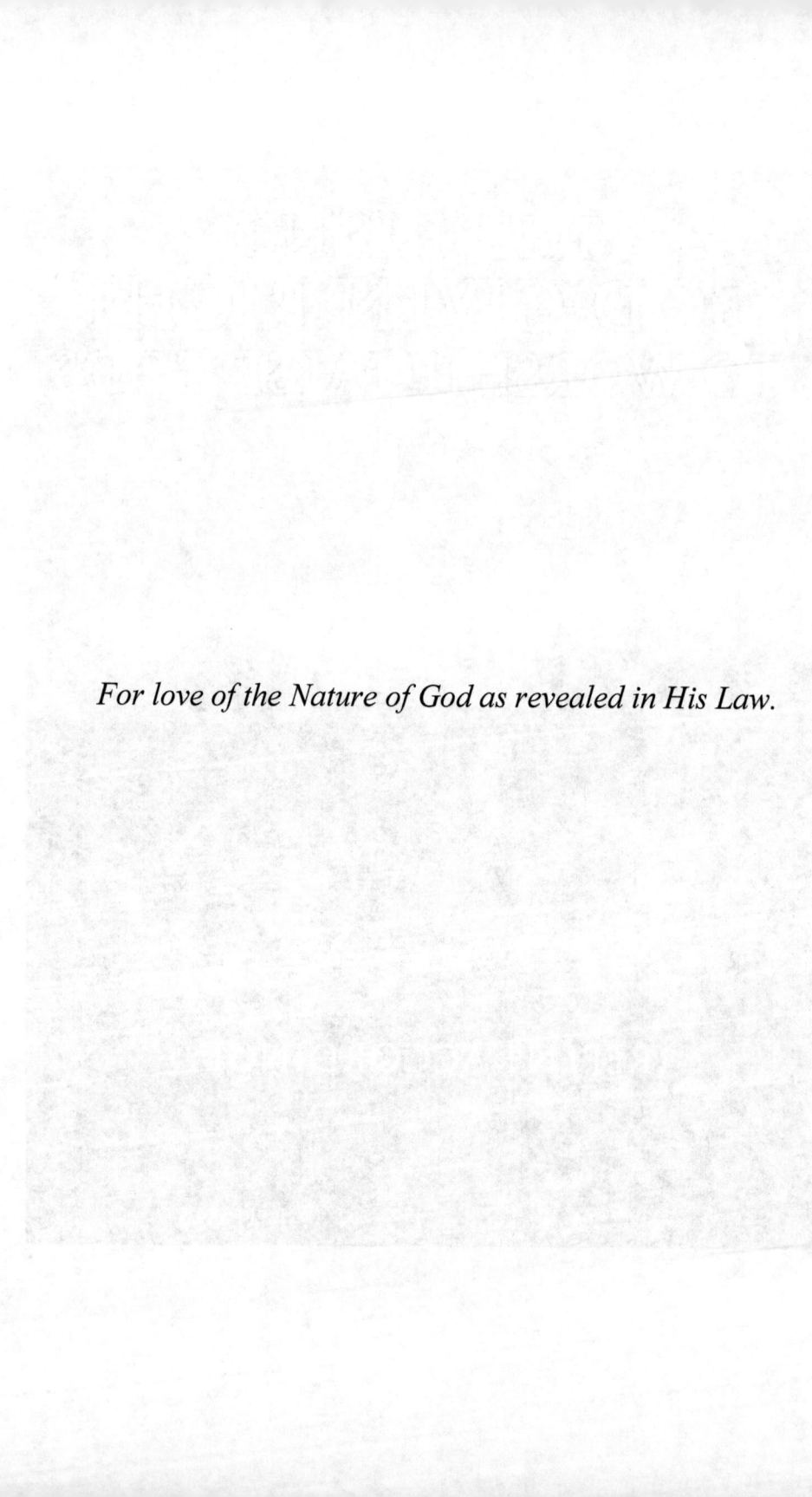

For love of the Nature of God as revealed in His Law.

THERE IS NO "GOD-GIVEN RIGHT" TO WORSHIP FALSE GODS
Contents

THERE IS NO "GOD-GIVEN RIGHT" TO WORSHIP FALSE GODS
Contents

THERE IS NO "GOD-GIVEN RIGHT" TO WORSHIP FALSE GODS
Contents

Our Suicidal Insanity

I can remember how surreal it felt the first time I saw the phrase in print:

"There is no 'God-given right' to worship false gods."

I'd been working through a short blog post on the subject of religious liberty and after writing that one little sentence I had to stop for a double take.

And then a triple.

For me it was a worldview shaking moment. It was weird and very challenging...but kinda cool at the same time. Even though I'd already been thinking on the subject since I was in the process of writing on it, there was something particularly heavy about that one simple phrase. It was, and is, such a sharp rebuke of the "religious liberty" concept we've been immersed in and encouraged to champion as Americans for as long as I've been alive and for many generations before I ever hit the scene.

Since being hit with that worldview-rocking revelation, it's been a mission of mine at *Fire Breathing Christian* to confront and correct the profoundly anti-Christian core of what we've been conditioned to embrace as "religious liberty" in America and throughout the West.

Since beginning to clearly proclaim and share this concept - the notion that there really is no "God-given right" to openly worship any false God anywhere in God's creation - I've been blessed to see and hear of eyes being opened, minds being renewed, and worldviews being reformed to embrace the biblical, explicitly Christ-centered gift of true religious liberty while repenting of and opposing the flagrantly anti-Christian counterfeit version that has become a crown jewel of the modern American identity and worldview.

My hope and prayer is that these articles will help Brothers and Sisters in Christ to see where idolatry has been encouraged and Scripture has been swept aside in the past so that we might, by God's grace, repent and reform our lives, families, churches, and culture.

All things must be centered clearly on the Nature of God as revealed in His Word if they are to be understood, pursued, and applied rightly - and by "rightly" I mean in a manner that leads to true life, joy, security, and prosperity as defined by God's Nature as revealed in His Word.

To look anywhere other than God for true knowledge about anything that He has made is to court chaos and pursue insanity...which is exactly what we have been doing for a very long time now in America and throughout the West.

Since this book is a compilation of distinct short articles centering on related subject matter, there will be a whole lot of overlap and repetition. Your patience in this regard is much appreciated.

One advantage of this format is that the reader will be able to jump around or take in an article or two as time permits without being overly concerned about context from one article to the next. While context will be clarified as more articles are read, they were originally presented as standalone items, so please feel free to take them in as such here.

I trust that the Lord will shake, convict, and inspire others as He has me through the simple declaration that "There is no 'God-given right' to worship false gods."

Thank you for your thoughtful consideration of these hard and often convicting things.

I hope and pray that He will forge my sometimes weak and wobbly use of words into a mighty weapon by which our most cherished of American idols might be exposed and crushed underfoot, so that we might finally pursue and find *true* freedom and liberty in America and everywhere else, all by God's grace, all for His glory, and all to our eternal benefit.

1
SECTION ONE

God-given Law
and
God-given Rights

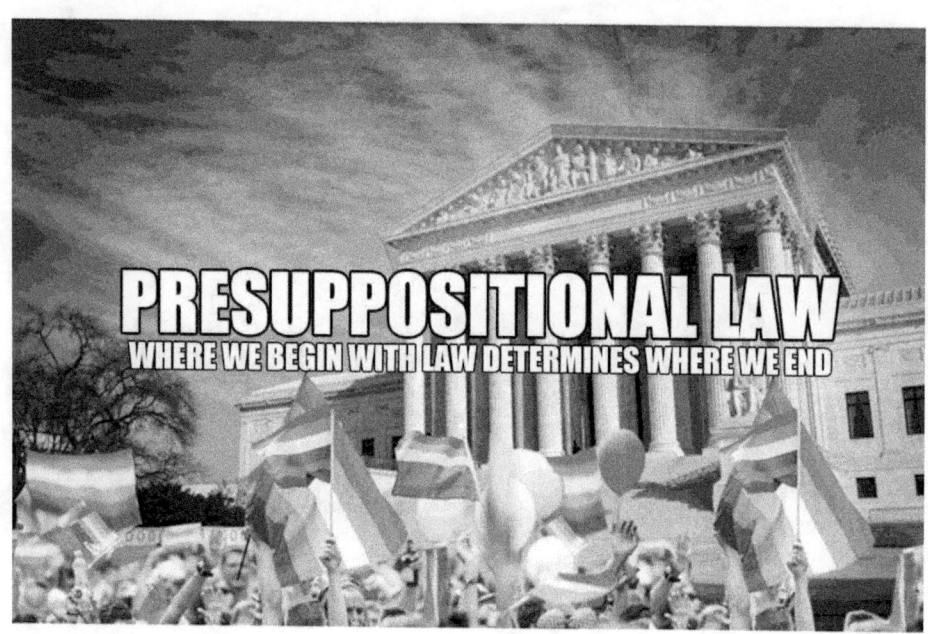

Presuppositional Law: Where we begin with law determines where we end.

(Originally published at *Fire Breathing Christian* on July 27, 2015.)

What is law?

What is the basis for law?

What ultimately determines whether a thing is lawful or lawless?

What we often automatically and unconsciously *presuppose* about the origin and nature of law determines what we will allow ourselves to see and consider from that point forward. Our *presuppositions* about the essence of law dictate which "truths" we will acknowledge as legitimate and which "realities" we will allow on our radar.

Where we *really* begin with our consideration of law is fundamental to where we will allow ourselves to go (and be taken) in pursuit of answers. The same goes for family, marriage, liberty, freedom, and life itself. That's just how things work in God's creation. Always has been. Always will be. There are no exceptions and there is no workaround. *Everything* in His creation is bound and defined by His Nature as revealed in His Word, whether or not we believe it, acknowledge it, or like it.

Law, as with all other things in the created universe, can only begin to be rightly understood by going to *the* beginning:

In the beginning, God created . . .

~ Genesis 1:1a

*For by him **all** things were created, in heaven and on earth, **visible and invisible**, whether thrones or dominions or rulers or authorities—**all things were created through him and for him**. And he is before all things, and **in him all things hold together**.*

~ Colossians 1:16-17 (bold emphasis added)

7

So it is that we understand that law is not a creation or invention of man. Law is not something that man can tweak or modify as he sees fit apart from the Nature of God as revealed in His Word.

Law belongs to God. It is a reflection of Him in His creation. It is born from, bound to, defined by and dependent upon His Nature.

Only with this simple but profound and essential truth in hand and held tight are we are able to rightly understand and apply law in God's creation.

But we aren't really encouraged to think of law this way, are we?

Of course not.

Every unbelieving "expert" and "leader" in the land – be they of a Pagan Political Right or Pagan Political Left flavor – is all about promoting and reinforcing the notion that law is *man's* and that any consideration of law here "in the real world" must begin with the assumption – the *presupposition* – that man is somehow, some way legitimately empowered and entitled to determine for himself what is lawful and what is lawless.

What could be more American than that?

And what could more quickly and easily provide clarity as to why our culture is spiraling into oblivion before our lawless, unbelieving little eyes?

What else could we have ever expected from a land proudly and defiantly built upon the "virtue" of religious pluralism? What else could have ever come to any land whose people claim the "right" (*God-given*, even) to openly worship false gods?

How could any people so proudly consecrated to the promotion of religious pluralism produce anything better than "legal" child sacrifice and "gay marriage" at the end of the day?

Why would we expect any more or any better from a "land of the free" where "freedom" includes the "right" to openly worship Satan?

This is where law leads when we *presuppose* it to be man's plaything.

This is what law becomes when we imagine it to be anything other than wholly reliant upon the Nature of God as revealed in His Word.

This is the lesson of America…a lesson that the Church is well served to note and apply as we move forward through this temporary wreckage and toward the supernatural victories and restoration to come, all by His grace, all for His glory, and all to the eternal benefit of His people.

Note to 'Merica: There is no "God-given right" to worship false gods. Repent accordingly.

(Originally published at *Fire Breathing Christian* on May 28, 2015.)

This may be news to most American "Christians" and most, if not all, of the "conservative Christian" Presidential candidates that they are likely to overwhelmingly support in the latest Pagan Right pitch to "save America", but, believe it or not: **There is no "God-given right" to openly worship false gods**.

While we're on the subject, it's probably also important to note that "rights" are only as good (or as real) as the God giving 'em, and that the one and only true and living God actually *despises* and *forbids* the open worship of false gods *anywhere in His creation*.

And yes, His creation includes 'Merica.

'Merica doesn't own and therefore doesn't get to define how reality works in 'Merica.

'Mericans don't own and therefore don't get to define how reality works in 'Merica.

God owns 'Merica.

God defines – He *personifies* – reality, for 'Merica and all else in His creation.

He has said with crystal clarity that the open worship of false gods is *forbidden*.

We can either repent of our proud 'Merican rebellion in this regard, or we can *continue* to be crushed under the wrath of the living God that we proudly mock every time we claim to have "the right" to do that which He has explicitly forbidden.

Evidence of His wrath pouring down upon us is evident in every area of life: Family, politics, church, art, civil government, economics, law… It's impossible to miss.

Unless we are still infatuated with our sin and blinded by our pride.

The bondage and hell of Statism is the inevitable reward of our pride and rebellion, and even the most dull-minded among us can sense its coming. Yet all we seem to want to do at this point to fight the looming doom of anti-Christian Statism is – unbelievably – double down on "core American (and satanic) principles" like the "God-given right" to openly worship false gods.

May God – the real One – save America, by either breaking her into submission or breaking her into a million pieces...some of which may, by His grace, actually strive to obey Him as He has lovingly commanded.

2
SECTION TWO

Christian Enabled Witchcraft, Islam and Satanism

TRAINWRECK GOSPELS

MAKE

TRAINWRECK CULTURES

Should Muslims and Satanists be allowed to seek public office in America?

(Originally published at *Fire Breathing Christian* on September 25, 2015.)

Should an openly practicing Muslim be allowed to seek and hold office in America?

What about a Satanist? Should an openly practicing Satanist be allowed to seek and hold office in America?

If not, why not?

If so, should "We the People" be open to voting for them? What about those of us who claim Christ as Lord? Should we be open to voting for the Satanist, too?

While the pilgrims and Puritans of America's early days wouldn't have required more than two nanoseconds (tops) to reject such notions (and follow-up with an obviously much-needed presentation of the Gospel), these sorts of questions are being seriously considered at some length by many – including many professing Christians – in America in the wake of Presidential candidate Dr. Ben Carson saying on Sunday that he wouldn't support a Muslim for president, and the answers that most professing Christians in America are coming up with are decidedly…well…*not* Christian.

The Christian Post, among many others, observed that "he was wrong to say that."

Ted Cruz jumped in there too, citing the Constitution as the gold standard in determining whether open worshipers of false gods should be allowed to seek and secure leadership positions in America.

Then Doug Wilson chimed in, bringing some much needed sanity to the scene:

"As you may have seen, Ben Carson was asked if he could support a Muslim in the presidency. He said, no, absolutely not. Forget about it. He was then asked if he could support a Muslim in

Congress. He said that would depend on candidate, positions, etc. Now there are some internal tensions in those answers, but unpacking those is not my purpose today. In the uproar that followed, Ted Cruz observed that the Constitution says that there will be no religious test for holding office, and that he, Ted Cruz, is a constitutionalist. Unlike that Carson guy.

But this is simply to partake in the grand secularist muddle, and to do so magnificently, in high style. It confuses questions that ought to be kept distinct, and it separates things that ought to be kept as parts of an organic whole.

Carson was asked if *he* could support a Muslim in the presidency. He was *not* asked if a Muslim should be legally and constitutionally eligible for that office. The questions are entirely distinct. A man could, without contradiction, say no to the first and yes to the second. He could also say no to both, but he would then be applying his anti-Muslim views to two separate questions.

So the question before the house is not whether we should make it constitutionally forbidden for a follower of the prophet Mohamed to become president. The question is whether Ben Carson, given a Muslim running, would support that guy."

While all o' this Carson/Cruz/Potential-Muslim-President stuff is interesting and important on many levels, one thing we should hope and pray that American Christians will come to understand and embrace is that when God explicitly prohibits the open worship of false gods (like Allah, for example, or Satan, for another), He is not playing games. He is not making "a suggestion". He is telling us *how it is*; He is explaining reality to us as it actually exists *everywhere* in His creation…which just so happens to include America.

God is explaining to us that in His creation the open worship of false Gods is always destructive. It always leads to death. There are no exceptions. Thus, out of love for us, He gives us life-preserving clarity on the matter in His Word.

So when we ditch His Word and grab on to the notion of secular "religious pluralism" as a good and noble thing, we are both mocking God and begging for His wrath upon our land and culture.

When we embrace the idea that "We the People" are free to openly worship any god we like and that this is a great virtue that not only serves as a central pillar of our culture, but is also something that all other cultures in the world ought to be encouraged to emulate, we are both mocking God and begging for His wrath upon our land and culture...and the lands and cultures that follow our lead.

When we embrace *that* explicitly *anti*-Christian concept of "religious liberty" and hold it high, we are begging for our own destruction.

Potential Muslim or Satanist or [insert any particular anti-Christ religious category here] candidate-for-President questions are symptomatic. The fact that they are almost always asked in a context that *presumes* the legality of openly practicing Muslims or Satanists or whatever in America demonstrates that we have a far more profound and far more foundational problem on our hands...and we don't even know it.

The question that we *should* be asking – but are discouraged at every turn from even noticing, much less contemplating – is the question as to the true legality of the open worship of false gods in the first place. As in: What has God said about this? What has God said is legally allowed in His creation where the worship of false gods is concerned? What has He commanded in this regard? And what has He promised will result from rejection of His life-giving Word on the subject?

Put another way, will we now seek, repent, and submit to the crystal clear Word of God on this vital question?

Or will "We the People" continue to cling to our pride and rebellion, even as our America Idol disintegrates into chaos all around us?

Will we keep symptomatically chattering on and on about the symptoms of the symptoms of the symptoms of our fundamental rejection of the lordship of Christ?

Or will we cut to the chase, take the axe to the root, finally repent and submit to Christ as King *in practice*?

17

May God grace us with broken, humble repentance, submission, and the otherwise impossible restoration to follow…while there is yet time.

"If you love me, you will keep my commandments."

~ Jesus (the real One), in John 14:15

Why do we allow the open practice of Islam, witchcraft, and Satanism in America?

(Originally published at *Fire Breathing Christian* on September 11, 2015.)

One of the weirdest and most telltale signs that we've become a people completely disconnected from reality is the way that here in America, even most "conservative" professing Christians have come to cherish and defend the concept of *religious pluralism.*

The idea that we have the "God-given 'right'" to worship any god or practice any religion that we choose has become a defining jewel in America's crown of pride and self-delusion. The "freedom to worship" any god is a centerpiece of the American worldview and foundational to America's identity...which pretty much explains in a nutshell why we are where we are now as a culture.

Even our favored conservative "experts" and "leaders", while almost always *claiming* Christianity, nonetheless relentlessly lead us along this path of religious pluralism, encouraging us to "stand up for the 'religious liberty'" upon which America was built and upon which it must stand.

[insert "*U! S! A!*" chant here]

Even as we commemorate the 9/11 attacks we are now encouraged by our "conservative Christian" leaders to defend and enable the "God-given 'right'" to open propagation of Islam and Muslim worship in America. The question begging to be asked here is: "So *which* 'God' gave us *this* 'right'?" If America is serving a god in all of this propagation of religious pluralism, it sure *isn't* the God of Christianity.

Even so, all of this defense and adoration of "religious liberty" (and therefore the many (infinite) *other* gods empowered by it) is relentlessly pitched as a basic duty of all good and properly patriotic Americans. "Religious liberty" must be defended no matter the cost...literally...

After all, this is the same "religious liberty" we must as good conservative Americans defend for **witches**.

19

And it's the same "religious liberty" that we good conservative American patriots must protect for **Satanists**.

You know, *that* "religious liberty".

Is anyone else's head spinning yet?

Is anyone else hearing *Twilight Zone* music?

And what does God – the *real* One – have to say about this All-American and uber-*patriotic* approach to religious liberty? What does **He** say about allowing the open worship of false gods in the land? What has **He** prescribed where the worship of false gods is concerned?

Do "We the People" even care?

Well, whether we care or not or like it or not, He *has* spoken, and with clarity:

> *And God spoke all these words, saying,*
> *"I am the LORD your God, who brought you out of the land of*
> *Egypt, out of the house of slavery.*
> ***You shall have no other gods before me.***"
>
> ~ Exodus 20:1-3 (emphasis added)

You may recognize this as number one of The Ten Commandments, found in Bibles as well as on all sorts of publicly displayed monuments, plaques, and statues *fiercely defended* (the statues; *not* the actual commandments) by "conservative Christians" all across the fruited plain...while the very same people automatically dismiss and openly trample the very commandment from God that is at the top the list.

When God says that we are to "have no other gods before" Him, He is not saying that other gods are okay as long as they're not placed above or beside Him. That's not the idea being expressed here at all. This is not God making an argument for a hierarchy of false gods that is somehow acceptable so long as we place Him atop the pile in some *symbolic* way. **That is a *wildly blasphemous* (and *very* American) concept.**

What God is explicitly condemning is <u>the presence of any false gods in His sight</u>. He is forbidding in the clearest language possible – here and throughout all of Scripture – the worship

of __any__ and __all__ false Gods. __He is specifically telling us that we cannot allow the open worship of false gods in our land__. To allow for such open worship of false gods is to mock the one true God and __beg for His wrath__.

Which brings us to America.

Here in the "land of the free" and home of the NSA, we're all about the proud adoration and defense of our "right" do to *exactly* that which God has explicitly condemned and forbidden, namely: Openly worship *any* god we like.

So the next time you're "wondering" why we've completely come off the rails and are now proudly (and suicidally) proclaiming the "legality" of "gay marriage" and the long-running "legality" of child sacrifice in the name of convenience and profit, please understand that there's no need to wonder. There's no real basis for confusion here. This is not some great baffling mystery requiring some supernaturally empowered Columbo or Perry Mason to figure out.

__We have deteriorated to this level over the past 200+ years – with the rate and trajectory of our decline increasing greatly as we go along – because we have first disregarded the crystal command of God to forbid the open worship of false gods in our land.__

I know, I know…this all sounds so very *un-American* of me…which is precisely the point.

When "conservative Christian" wannabe "leaders" and "experts" like Mike Huckabee, Ben Carson, and every other Pagan Right Wing political advocate try to woo (as they always do) conservative Christians with appeals to the importance of "religious liberty" (__by which they *always* mean religious pluralism, which God despises__), they are leading us deeper and deeper into darkness and ruin.

Got it?

Please get it…

I know it's hard. I know it's challenging. I know it grates against the All-American core we've been programmed to embrace since toddlerhood through State- and Corporate-owned "education" systems and pop culture, but *we have to shake off the lies*. The hour is late and it's getting darker by the second. **We really need to take hold of this hard truth and repent accordingly.**

Right now…while there is still time.

Which "god" would grant the "right" to openly worship Satan? Hmmm...I wonder...

(Originally published at *Fire Breathing Christian* on September 23, 2015.)

Even *Saturday Night Live* is ultimately God's tool.

Yes, really.

Even something like a foolish, mocking swipe at Christ and His Bride, the Church, when taken by the likes of *SNL,* is *always* ultimately going to be used perfectly by God for His glory to accomplish His purposes for the benefit of His people (see: Romans 8:28).

With that beautiful, unbreakable truth duly noted (and while also noting that this is in no way an endorsement of *SNL* on my part), let's have a look at just one way in which one of this popular show's anti-Christian presentations can now be seen and applied in a very helpful manner.

Back in the late '80s, NBC's *Saturday Night Live* featured a recurring segment called *Church Chat* starring Dana Carvey as The Church Lady, a tightly wound, condescending, hyper-puritanical granny-like critic who saw Satan behind every curtain, around every corner, and under every carpet. Episodes of *Church Chat* would culminate with The Church Lady rhetorically musing and building her case as to who was *really* behind whatever "terrible thing" she had in her sights on that particular weekend. She'd wonder and speculate as to "who, oh who(?!)" could *possibly* be the *real* power behind the evil of Halloween or Santa Claus or Hollywood or whatever.

"*Who* oh *who* could it ***possibly*** be?!

Hmmm...I just don't know...who could *possibly* be behind such flagrant acts of darkness?

Could it just *maybe* possibly be...

...*SATAN*!!!"

That's where The Church Lady would lead America on Saturday nights.

Church Chat would lead the culture laughingly down a Christianity-parodying, Christ-dismissing, Satan-minimalizing path – a path that, it should be noted – was originally cleared and has since been well maintained by professing Christians who've embraced practically every unbiblical stereotype of the Christian life and have lived down to every secular caricature imaginable.

Church Chat and The Church Lady are first and foremost byproducts of the actual Church's surrender to Satan-empowering, *Left Behind*-style "end times" views and rejection of the Gospel-fueled Great Commission. *Church Chat* is what happens when the Church is known primarily as a bunch of disengaged, monochromatic dinosaurs who have little desire to take art, science, humor, technology, law and the like "captive to Christ" (2 Corinthians 10:5) and instead prefer to play the role of self-righteous sideline sniper while hunkering down and waiting for the rapture.

While there's a lot in there to think about and much that may be worth kicking around in future posts and podcasts, what we're gonna focus on now is one area in which The Church Lady actually (and ironically and sadly) seems to have a leg up on the Church.

By "the Church" here I mean the *professing* Church in America.

And by "a leg up", I mean this:

Imagine, if you will, a new episode of *Church Chat* in which The Church Lady considers the notion of "religious liberty" as currently adored, defended, and aggressively promoted by pretty much every System-enabled American "leader" and "expert", including every national level talking head from the Pagan Political Right, the Pagan Political Left, and all Pagan Political points in between.

Imagine The Church Lady concluding her presentation with…:

"Now who, oh **who**, I wonder, would *ever* be behind such a thing as the "right" to *openly worship false gods*? Hrmmm…I wonder who *that* would be…

Who could *possibly* be behind such an idea?

24

Who could *possibly* be behind the notion of a **"god-given 'right'"** to openly worship false gods in America?

Hmmmm…

Exactly which "god" or wannabe god would propose such a thing, I wonder?

Who could it possibly be?

Could it perhaps just **maybe** be…

SATAN?!!!"

And there we have it: The most obvious answer to what has to qualify as some of the easiest to answer series of questions in all of recorded history.

The most obvious would-be "god" who would happily and purposefully champion the notion of a "God-given 'right'" to openly worship false gods in America (or anywhere else) is Satan.

No kidding!

What a stunner!

Who could have ever missed this, right?

I mean, what could be more obvious than the satanic foundation and inspiration of the "religious liberty" and "God-given 'right'" to openly worship false gods (like Satan) in America?

Well…if you've been "educated" by the American State for the benefit of the American State in the American State's chosen religion of *Statism*, you've probably managed to miss this rather glaring (and kind of important) truth.

Moreover, if you've been as thoroughly programmed and conditioned by State and Corporate owned schools and pop culture as the typical professing Christian in America, you probably view what I'm doing in daring to criticize the All-American notion of "religious liberty" as the real blasphemy here. You may have even, at the behest of your favorite Pagan Political Right "leader" or "expert" recently joined in a rally defending the "religious liberty" and "rights" of Muslims and Satanists to openly worship Allah or Satan in America, having been led to believe that this is somehow "the good Christian thing to do".

And you've probably also been led down this path by your very own "conservative, Bible-believing" pastor or priest.

Do you now see how far we've fallen?

Do you see how desperate our condition really is?

We have a lot of work to do.

But before that work can really, truly begin, we have a lot of *repenting* to do.

We have a lot of Pagan/satanic thought to purge.

We have a lot of Pagan/satanic "leaders" and "experts" to reject and oppose.

We have a lot of rebuilding and restoring to do by casting down our pride and taking up the long-rejected Gospel-fueled Great Commission, doing what our Lord has *commanded* and *equipped* us to do, all by His grace, all for His glory, and all to our eternal benefit (see: Matthew 28:18-20).

Only then will the professing Christian Church in America become *less ridiculous* and *less destructive* than *Church Chat* and The Church Lady.

Only then will we not only recognize but **crush** the wannabe god behind the supposed "freedom" to worship Allah or Satan anywhere in God's creation.

Christians rally for the "rights" of Satanists to worship Satan in America.

(Originally published at *Fire Breathing Christian* on September 18, 2015.)

Interesting and important conversations are taking place in America.

Critical and challenging thoughts are being entertained in a serious way by many Americans for the first time in a good long while (if ever).

We are now being forced, by the grace of God, to consider what it means exactly to worship and what it means to have liberty to worship in a land like America (or any other in His creation). We are being forced to choose between a thoroughly satanic – and very All-American – approach to the concept of religious liberty, and a biblical approach to the same. We are being forced to choose this day whom we will serve and worship – and who we will allow to be openly served and worshiped – in America.

Put another way: We are being forced to "test all things", including our most cherished traditions and thoroughly engrained assumptions about patriotism, freedom, worship and liberty by the pure light of the perfect Word of God.

And what we are being shown in that perfect Light is hard. *Very* hard for us as proud Americans.

It's extremely challenging.

And it's *purposefully* rocking our culture to its core...right on time. (Again, never forget: All of this is happening in precise compliance with God's perfect, and perfectly *set*, schedule.)

The subject of "religious liberty" is now front and center in the minds of many Americans.

That's the good news.

And before we get to the bad news, let's add a little more good: More and more Christians are finally beginning to awaken to the reality that the "religious liberty" concept they've been pitched, sold, and led to embrace as good, patriotic, "conservative Christian" Americans for their entire lives is, in fact, a lie.

27

A thoroughly satanic lie, to be more precise.

The bad news is that the vast majority of politically active "conservative" professing Christians are still very much ensnared of this lie, to the point that they adore it, cherish it, and vigorously defend it any time it is criticized, even when criticism brought in perfect harmony and accordance with the Christian command to "test all things" and "take every thought" – including every political, legal, and governmental thought – "captive to Christ" (see: 1 Thessalonians 5:21 and 2 Corinthians 10:5).

Yesterday I had the opportunity to visit a "religious liberty" rally and mingle with folks there. These are "my kind of people" in so many ways and I sympathize with 'em on many levels. Passionately so. This is what makes it so very painful to see so many professing Christians coming together not to stand for biblical religious liberty, but rather for the satanic counterfeit. This is what makes it so heartbreaking to see so many Brothers and Sisters still profoundly misled and misleading others to actually and quite vigorously champion the "right" of a Satanist to worship Satan in America.

Just think about that.

Test it.

Test it first to see if it is simply true, which it is. The Pagan American "religious liberty" construct as actually crafted and applied has led us to where we are now, with mosques, covens, and "churches of satan" operating quite openly and with full "legal" protection all across the "land of the free" and home of the self-described "brave" (not surprisingly alongside equally "legally protected" baby butchering "clinics", it should be noted.)

Ask the typical professing Christian "conservative" at one of these events if we as Americans have and *must vigorously defend* the right to worship *any* god we like or practice *any* religion we like, and they will heartily amen while waving their flag...the flag of their true god *in practice* on the subject of religious liberty.

This "liberty", they will almost always admit, must, of necessity, cover groups that we may not like or with whom we may disagree...like Islam and Satanism, for example.

That's the supposedly "God-given 'right' to 'religious liberty'" that we're supposed to unquestioningly champion and revere here in America.

Which "god" would actually grant such a "right" if he could, I wonder? (I mean *besides* the "god" of America.)

What "god", exactly, would presume to authorize and promote the "right" to worship Allah, Satan, or whatever other life-destroying lie one might be inclined to follow?

Which "god" would presume to grant and encourage vigorous defense of the "right" to openly worship these false gods?

Which "god" would dare prescribe as a "right" that which the one *true* God has explicitly condemned and forbidden?

[insert Church Lady voice here]

Hmmm…

Oh, I dunno…

could it be…

…*Satan*?!)

[/end Church Lady voice]

But nobody in America seems to notice, much less care. That's how far we've been led down the path of America as god in practice and unthinking patriotism as our preferred religion.

So the rallies go on.

Throngs and throngs of "conservatives" gather to passionately proclaim and defend the "right" of Muslims to openly worship Allah and Satanists to openly worship Satan in America.

The devil laughs.

The culture burns.

With "American Christians" leading the way, as usual.

Mosques over America: Will we live by the First Commandment or die by the First Amendment?

(Originally published at *Fire Breathing Christian* on October 23, 2014.)

One of the more memorable moments in Cecil B. Demille's *The Ten Commandments* comes when Charlton Heston – I mean, *Moses* – comes down from Mount Sinai with the Ten Commandments of God to man. He makes this dramatic return after a long absence during which the people of Israel engaged in rank idolatry and open rebellion against their Creator.

So ~~Chuck~~ Moses comes on down from the mountain where he has been communing with God, sees that things have gone terribly wrong with his people, and commands them to obey the Lord and His commandments, which he just happens to have right there with him on two stone tablets. The movie line that sticks with me (and no doubt many others) to this very day comes after a few heed Moses' call to repentance while many do not. There is a divide in the camp of Israel, and after the few who seek the Lord come to Moses' side, he announces to the multitude that, "Those who will not live by the law shall die by the law!"

As Christians, we understand that Christ has lived the obedient life that we never could and that He has done so on our behalf, laying Himself down as a sacrifice for our disobedience so that we are no longer "under the law" as the standard by which we must personally earn, attain, or maintain salvation. One of the great, beautiful truths of the Gospel is that our salvation comes by grace alone through faith alone in Christ alone, who is the embodiment of the Law, the Word Made flesh, and who loved the Law faithfully and perfectly, all to our account. That is how much Christ the King loves both the Law and the people for whom He died.

Again and again, Scripture provides us with the way by which we can test our faith; the means by which we can answer the question, "Am I really saved?" And each and every time, the answer has to do with

31

testing our profession of love for Christ against our desire for obedience to all that He has commanded *in practice*.

One great, bold, and crystal clear dividing line between true Christians – those who have been supernaturally saved and transformed into New Creatures in Christ – and all other people, however much they may claim Christ or Christianity through their lips, religion, and traditions, is this: Those who are truly saved by Him *will* have, *by His grace through His Spirit within them*, a thirst, desire, and reverence for His commandments. They will desire to know about His law and commandments more and more clearly because they want to know *Him* more and more clearly, and they recognize that *His Word and Law are revelations of His personal Nature*. They are part of who He is. Therefore His people *will* seek repentance as they learn more and more about their sin through the revelation of His nature through His Word and His Law. And they *will* – again, *all by His grace* – each personally strive to *apply* His Word in *every* realm of their lives. Right here and right now. That is the Gospel and Great Commission on *active display*. That is true Christianity *in practice*...all by His grace and for His glory.

And that is precisely the opposite of what is pitched and preached in most "churches" in America.

Here again we see how true it is that both judgment and restoration always have and always will begin with God's people, the one true Church.

> *For it is time for judgment to begin at the household of God; and if it begins with us, what will be the outcome for those who do not obey the gospel of God?*
>
> ~ 1 Peter 4:17

American Christians Confronting American Idolatry

We face a stark choice at this moment in American history. Many stark choices, actually, but one rises head and shoulders above the rest, leaving all others in its inescapable shadow. That towering, culture- and civilization-defining choice is: *Will we repent and submit to Christ the King, or will we persist in proud rebellion and destroy ourselves upon His unbreakable Nature?*

The ongoing plagues and ever-increasing stream of crises that are even now ravaging our culture should be making this point plain, but they do not seem to be doing so. Thus far, Americans are, as they have done for many generations, looking everywhere *but* to the Nature of God as revealed in His Word as the standard by which to measure *everything* and confront *every* challenge. Instead, many rebels on the left look to the State, MSNBC, CNN, and the Democrat Party, while many church-going, Bible-reading rebels on the right seek first the advice of Rush Limbaugh, Mark Levin, Fox News, and the support of *their* favorite version of the State for "solutions" and a worldview to build their lives upon. They look to places where the Gospel and Great Commission commands of Christ the King are mocked through the disdainful act of *dismissal without comment,* as if they had the power or authority to deny the authority of Christ by simply *ignoring* Him.

What profound (and suicidally stupid) arrogance!

Such is the disdain of Fox News, CNN, the Republican Party, and the Democrat Party for the very nature of Jesus Christ.

They will *not* have Christ the King to rule over them. They will not even hear of such a thing! On this, Republicans and Democrats can agree. Church-going protestants, homosexual activists, successful businessmen and sweet old ladies can all agree: They will *not* submit *their* lives to *His* rule right here and now. They simply will not have it.

This is why these people are not only accustomed to "not hearing the Gospel" as a cornerstone of political, economic, or educational pursuits, but they like it that way. Their gospel, if they claim one, is neatly sequestered in "its place". It may be taken out on Sundays or during Bible studies or for certain conversations with certain people, but it is certainly not held close as the essential core of truth in every realm of life right here and now. No, *that* sort of gospel is *scary.* It's *fanatical.* It's *dangerous.*

And why is it dangerous?

Because it threatens *our* idols…

A Simple Test for Idolatry

"Get rid of mosques?! Ban Islamic worship?! But we *can't* do *that!*"

"This is *America!*"

"Here we are *free* – free to worship *any* god *any* way that we want!"

What do statements like these inspire in you?

Do you generally agree with them? Do you generally disagree? Do they make you proud? Do they make you sick?

Have you ever even thought about them in this context? Have you ever thought about them in light of the First Commandment, in which God *explicitly forbids allowing the worship of any pretend god in the land*?

I hadn't thought of these things this way for most of my life, but here I am now, by God's grace, trying to learn and submit to some initially hard, but ultimately beautiful truths, while hoping to encourage you to do the same.

I do this because I love America and I love you, knowing that I can only love America and love you rightly by first loving God rightly, on His terms as He has clearly presented and equipped His people to understand them.

I share these things now because we really are at a critical point in America. The hour is late. Judgment is upon us.

It is in this context that I ask, "By whose standard?"

By whose standard will we actively strive to live in *every* area of life?

Are some areas for God and others for man to define and determine?

Or is *everything* His?

Will we each personally put everything on the line and dedicate everything that we have been given by God to seek and apply His will in embrace of the true Gospel and obedience to the Great Commission?

Or will we do…something else…anything else…the details matter little in the end.

The right answer to these questions gives us all that we need to actively and successfully tackle the "big challenges" that can never and will never be soundly addressed by Fox News, Rush Limbaugh, Barack Obama, the Republicans, or the Democrats. When we repent of rebellion and pursue His Nature as lovingly revealed in His Word as the basis upon which we act in every realm of His creation, we can "do all things"…by His grace and for His glory.

When we choose any other path – any other worldview or approach to life, however adored and steeped in tradition it may be – we choose darkness and death.

That's how things actually work in "the real world".

His world.

Operating under *His* rules.

Defined and sustained by *His* unbreakable Nature as revealed in His perfect Word.

So, what do we do about Mosques and the open practice of Islam in America?

Do we continue tolerate it and exalt such tolerance as a virtue? Do we continue to proudly champion this virtue as a value for the whole world to embrace?

Or do we repent and believe…*in action?*

That is the question, America.

Or, put another way: Will we live by the First Commandment or die by the First Amendment?

Should "The Greater Church of Lucifer" be allowed to operate in America?

(Originally published at *Fire Breathing Christian* on October 9, 2015.)

"The Greater Church of Lucifer is celebrating its grand opening this month on Main Street. . . "

So begins the clinical, ho-hum, matter-of-fact intro from KPRC Channel 2 News' television segment this week on the new "church" opening in town.

The News 2 article provides some of the *very* American-friendly spin offered up by advocates of the new "church":

> "We do not have a preacher," No said. "We do not have somebody saying, 'This is the way it has to be, you have to live this way.'"
>
> Although some of their symbols may be disturbing to outsiders, leaders said they view Lucifer not in the Judeo-Christian view as the devil, but as a source of light that challenges people to think outside the box.
>
> For them, it's all about the individual.
>
> "We're giving a platform for people to explore themselves with ultimate freedom," No said. "They will be able to look in the mirror and say, 'I understand you better.'"
>
> The GCOL is scheduled to officially open on Oct. 30 and leaders say they are getting interest from people all over the world who want to attend that grand opening.

This is what satanic "freedom" looks like, and I'm not referring to the idiotic contentions of the sad little self worshippers advocating for the "Greater Church of Lucifer".

I'm talking about a country that would permit the open practice of such religion in the first place.

I'm talking about the suicidal idiocy of any people who think it good to allow, cherish, and defend something as destructively oxymoronic as a "God-given right to worship Lucifer"...or any other false god.

In other words, I'm talkin' 'bout 'Merica.

"The Greater Church of Lucifer" and every other openly operating mosque, temple, coven and the like is God's judgment upon a very proud and very doomed "We the People" who are so given over to the insanity described in Romans 1 that we *actually believe* that allowing such things is a sign of *virtue*.

When "We the People" simultaneously refuse to submit to the perfect Word of God in our approach to law and civil government while proudly championing the "God-given rights" of Americans to openly worship Allah and Satan, you know that the hour is very late and, apart from massive, sweeping repentance and submission to Christ as King in practice, the proud and unrepentant are soon to be removed from *His* land.

Woe to those who call evil good and good evil. . .
~ Isaiah 5:20

I will tell of the decree:
The LORD said to me, "You are my Son;
today I have begotten you.
*Ask of me, and **I will make the nations your heritage,***
and the ends of the earth your possession.
You shall break them with a rod of iron
and dash them in pieces like a potter's vessel."
Now therefore, O kings, be wise;
be warned, O rulers of the earth.
Serve the LORD with fear,
and rejoice with trembling.
Kiss the Son,
lest he be angry, and you perish in the way,
for his wrath is quickly kindled.
Blessed are all who take refuge in him.
~ Psalm 2:7-12 (emphasis added)

Islamic worship in American government? Sure. Why not?

(Originally published at *Fire Breathing Christian* on November 15, 2014.)

Is America all about the freedom to worship *any* god?

Of course!

Does America – including the vast majority of its self-identified "conservative Christians" – hold up this "right" as *a great and civilization-defining virtue* worthy of emulation by all other people in all other lands?

Of course!

Then what's the matter with an Islamic Imam formally and officially leading our nation's leadership in prayer to and worship of *a false god*?

The answer is: *Nothing*…if we simply take an honest, sober, consistent look at what America *actually* stands for when it comes to God, false gods, and worship.

The one true God of Christianity could not be more clear, simple, and plain in His disdain for that which we champion globally as our greatest virtue: the "right" to worship any god. (See: The Ten Commandments.)

And what is the American response to God's crystal clear command on this vital subject of the worship of false gods?

What has it been since the founding of our (once) Republic?

Something like, "Thanks for the advice, God, but we have a better idea. We think that allowing the worship of false gods is not only okay, but very important to *protect*."

God has spoken. He has given great clarity on this subject and forbids that we allow such evil to be openly pursued in public out of a love for us and a desire to protect us from the inevitable (and most serious) consequences of rebellion against Him. The first of the Ten Commandments – the commandment upon which all the rest are founded – could not be more plain.

Which makes America's rejection of God just as plain…however much our American idolatry may prevent us from acknowledging, much less repenting of, our great and glaring sin.

The latest in a long line of increasingly stark (yet likely to be ignored or deflected) examples this ongoing American rebellion was reported today in a post titled *Islamic Imam Leads U.S. House of Representatives in Prayer 'in the Name of Allah'*, published at ChristianNews.net, which informed us that, "An Islamic imam led the U.S. House of Representatives in prayer 'in the name of Allah' this week, as those representing the people from states across America stood with their heads bowed and eyes closed." The article continued:

> *Imam Hamad Ahmad Chebli of the Islamic Society of Central Jersey in Monmouth opened the day on Thursday, being introduced by Speaker John Boehner.*
> *"In the name of Allah, the most gracious, the most merciful," he began. "Praise be to Allah, the cherisher, the sustainer of the world, the most gracious, the most merciful master of the Day of Judgment. Thee do we worship and thine do we seek."*

With the larger historic context clearly understood, we can see that this week's formal, official worship by our government of a false god as led by an Islamic Imam was a destination charted long before anyone like Barack Obama hit the scene in Hawaii or Kenya or wherever. This should help to keep our eyes on the ball and prevent us from being manipulated by the distractions so frequently and effectively deployed by anti-Christian media from all points on the political spectrum. All of those anti-Christian sources – from MSNBC and CNN to FOX and Rush Limbaugh – take and present it as a given that the freedom to worship any false god is a great American virtue, and everything that they say on this or any related subject will be thoroughly rooted in and defined by that completely anti-Christian perspective. Never forget that.

And never forget that the seed for this particular "grand demonstration of the beautiful freedom to worship false gods" – this flagrant display of disdain for the one true God – was planted in the earliest years of US history, and it was planted by none other than the iconic untouchables of modern American "conservative-first Christianity": The Founding Fathers.

In our flight from God as Lord in practice and His Word as our standard for all things in practice, The Founding Fathers have become the gold standard for law-givers in America, and the Constitution has become the gold standard for law, even in the minds and worldviews of most professing Christians. Rather than testing and reforming everything – including politics and economics – by biblical standards, we have become a proud nation of, by, and for *man-centeredness*. We have become unified in proud rebellion against the inescapable, unbreakable lordship of Christ.

This is why we worship false gods openly, officially and proudly...all while daring to pretend aloud at the same time that we are doing so using a "right" that has been given us by the very God who has explicitly condemned the very thing that we are doing.

Put another way, we have been "given over" to insanity (see: Romans 1).

In our idolatry of *ourselves* – our nation, our flag, our patriotism, and our Founding Fathers – we have separated the object of our affection (again: ourselves) from the one and only true source of life, liberty, prosperity and happiness.

May God break us of this insanity. May He break us of our pride. May He do whatever is required to bring us to happily, truthfully, and completely submit to Him as the one and only true source of every good thing anywhere in His creation. May His people be graced with the desire and opportunity to stand completely for His Gospel and Great Commission in this dark hour.

Why using the Ten Commandments as a lucky rabbit's foot is a really bad idea.

(Originally published at *Fire Breathing Christian* on July 2, 2015.)

Contrary to popular American mythology, things like Bibles and Ten Commandments monuments make lousy (and particularly blasphemous) lucky rabbits' feet.

When we use them as superstitious icons and trinkets of protection – as we routinely do here in "the land of the free" and the home of the NSA – we aren't proclaiming our fidelity to God and we certainly aren't honoring God. We're actually heaping additional judgment upon our heads and begging for His wrath upon us.

When we sprinkle Bibles or Ten Commandments plaques around our *openly anti-Christian,* State-run schools and government complexes, such religious trinkets do not somehow magically transform those wildly unbiblical institutions into something God-honoring or good. The main thing that these superstitious icons accomplish is the clear revelation of our disinterest in *applying* what those Bibles and Commandments *command*.

By taking this religious/superstitious trinket approach to God and His Word, we've demonstrated in a uniquely powerful and blasphemous manner that we know that His Word exists…and we just don't care.

Oh, we care enough to keep it around for its *ornamental* value. But as the means by which we actually understand and pursue life in detail? Not so much.

We're gonna do things *our* way.

We're gonna do children's education *our* way.

We're gonna do economics and business *our* way.

We're gonna do law and justice and civil government *our* way.

We're America!

Besides, so long as we get our tickets to heaven punched by claiming Jesus as Lord with our lips, what's all the fuss? Why stress about actually *doing* what Jesus has commanded?

"We the people" have the "right" to do what *we* think is best 'round here, and it'll all work out in the end, 'cause, um…*we're 'Merica!*

So *what* if our economic foundation is wildly unbiblical and is therefore being purposefully used to lead us into ever-increasing subjugation and slavery to the American Corporate State?

So *what* if our legal and political foundations are wildly unbiblical and are therefore being used to lead us deeper and deeper into the hell of full-blown Statism and the total loss of true freedom, liberty and privacy?

So *what* if our military and foreign policy foundations are so flagrantly anti-Christian that they are being successfully used to lead us into perpetual war overseas while justifying the perpetual loss of freedom at home?

So *what* if our foundations for business and work are so thoroughly unbiblical that even most hard working Americans are increasingly dependent upon the American Corporate State and obedient Christians are being increasingly persecuted into silence and submission to that American State's pro-gay, anti-Christian agenda?

So *what* if our foundation for civil government is so perverse and radically unbiblical that "we the people" are no longer even allowed to own homes here in "the land of the free" and the home of the NSA?

So *what* if our American concepts of "freedom", "liberty", "truth", "justice" and even "life" itself are so self-servingly vile and rank that we are able to – *in the name of freedom and liberty* – abide by the open, systematic mass murder of our own children, sacrificed by the tens-of-millions on the twin altars of *convenience* and *profit*?

How obvious should things be at this point?

How glaring are the consequences of our rebellion against the *content* of the Law and Bibles that we freely and superstitiously sprinkle around the countryside in the magical fairytale hope that their mere physical presence will somehow help to blunt (and maybe even *reverse*) the mind-blowing cultural carnage unfolding before our selfish, unbelieving little eyes?

By planting plaques and posters and monuments to God's Word and Law all around us while simultaneously refusing to actually *read* and **submit to** His Word in the way that we pursue things like law, children's education and civil government, we demonstrate our contempt for God and His Word on a level far more profound than those "non-Christian" nations that we proudly imagine ourselves to be worthy of lecturing on things like truth, justice and the 'Merican way.

So when religious trinkets like the Ten Commandments monument at the Oklahoma state capitol are ordered to be removed, as recently reported, we shouldn't be so quick to protest. We should perhaps be thankful for the consistent application of our proud American culture's insane commitment to religious pluralism (as a "God-given right", no less), so that we might more clearly see the unbreakable truth of God's Law and **repent of our long and proud rebellion against it**.

It is *our contempt* for His Word that has led us to our present condition.

It is *our contempt* for His Word that has Islamic prayers openly promoted in our civil government.

It is *our contempt* for His Word that has *witches* leading official prayers in our civil governmental bodies.

It is *our contempt* for His Word that has Islamic mosques operating openly all over the land.

It is *our contempt* for His Word that has the homosexual deathstyle advancing like a tidal wave over the culture.

It is *our contempt* for His Word that has millions of *our own little children* freely sacrificed on the altar of convenience both unto death at abortuaries and unto lives of State-programmed Corporate servitude in "education" systems built upon an approach to the pursuit of knowledge yanked from serpent's tongue in Eden.

So let's stop getting all wound up about having Ten Commandments *plaques* on display here or there, or allowing students to tote around Bibles as they go about their daily immersion in explicitly anti-Christian instruction.

Let's actually *do* what those ornamental plaques, monuments, and Bibles command us to do in the realms of law, education, economics and everywhere else, right here and now, while there is still time.

America's "freedom" to murder children and worship false gods.

(Originally published at *Fire Breathing Christian* on April 8, 2015.)

Child sacrifice is about as ugly – and as American – as it gets.

With "we the people" as god *in practice*, and Christ the King utterly disregarded whenever His crystal clear commands conflict with the desires, traditions and *feelings* of that god, we have for generations been proudly set upon a sure path to the wildest of blasphemies and most horrific of atrocities.

As of right now, it looks like we're at least approaching the end of that path. After generations of material prosperity and relative strength on the world stage being mistaken for (and proudly paraded about as) the blessing and favor of the one true God, our cumulative rebellion against His Nature as revealed in His Word is finally beginning to come into full bloom.

A recent Breitbart report chronicled one of many recent steps into our special little American "liberty"-fueled hell. The article, *University of Hawaii Carrying Out Controversial Abortion Experiments on Minors*, relayed the horrifying – yet entirely predictable – news that the University of Hawaii "is currently recruiting pregnant girls and women to participate in second-trimester abortions to measure their bleeding during the operation, with and without antihemorrhagic drugs. According to the Clinical Trials website, run by the National Institutes of Health, participants must be at least 14 years old and 18-24 weeks pregnant."

Is this disgusting?

Yes.

Is it repulsive?

Of course.

Is it wicked, vile, and evil?

Yes, yes, and yes.

It is all of these things, to be sure, but it is no less *American*.

47

Child sacrifice is what we do.

We do it more systematically, more openly, and more proudly than *any* other people at any time in human history. We murder children with a cool, calm callousness that would make Mao wince, and we sacrifice children to the Corporate State with a happy compliance that would make Joseph Goebbels weep with jealousy.

There can be no doubt: When it comes to child sacrifice at every level, we're #1! We're 'Merica!

[insert "*U! S! A!*" chant here]

Each and every year here in the "land of the free" and the home of the NSA, we literally feed millions of our own children into the woodchipper of an American Corporate State sanctioned, publicly displayed system of mass murder and dismemberment that would make Dr. Mengele blush and the average Nazi's head spin. Those lucky kiddos who manage to avoid said woodchipper are then quite likely to be happily sacrificed (even by professing Christian parents) to the Corporate State through submission to an anti-Christ "education" system whose foundation and worldview is lifted straight from the serpent's tongue.

So yeah, it's pretty bad.

And how did we get here? What happened to make all of this not only possible, but assured?

We rebelled against God…and loved it!

Somewhere between the Puritans and the Founders, we went off the rails in fundamental ways. Somewhere along the way – before even the formal foundation of the United States – we started down a path that would lead us to embrace as legitimate one of the most obvious, glaring, and destructive prohibitions in Scripture: The worship of false gods.

The enshrinement of the "right" to worship any god as both a *God*-given thing and an All-American *virtue* constitutes a remarkable conflagration of high rebellion concepts, when you stop and think about it biblically. There are so many ways in which this most cherished of Americanisms is an affront to God that it's hard to list them all.

The nature of our problem can – as always – be found in our rejection of the Nature of God – more specifically, in our rejection of His Nature as revealed in His perfect, sufficient Word.

Once we decided that His Nature was not the actual, detailed basis for things like law, culture, and civilization, we were doomed to our present-day condition and the much worse that is right around the corner.

Just as our rejection of His revealed Nature as the basis for everything including law and government is the single gate through which all of our present misery and corruption has marched, so too is our broken, repentant return and submission to His Word in detail and practice our only hope.

That is the only answer.

Because *He* is the only answer.

Every political pundit, expert, party, and politician pointing to anyone or anything *but* Him as a real solution is only leading us further down the path to cultural oblivion and the inevitable subsequent tyranny of Statism.

There is no true law apart from His *personal* Nature. One way or another – either through our persistent pride and American idolatry or our broken repentance and submission to Christ as King in practice – we will validate His unbreakable Nature. We will confirm His unbreakable Word. America will come and go, but the Kingdom and people of God will endure forever, all by His grace and for His glory.

His Nature as defined in His Word is not optional to life. It is essential to life.

Until and unless we are moved en mass by His grace to repent and embrace that life-enabling truth, we are as doomed as the children we sacrifice by the millions as a matter of daily routine here in the "land of the free" known as America.

49

Prancing Ponies, Bible Belt Satanists, and America's Proud Rebellion

(Originally published at *Fire Breathing Christian* on December 12, 2013.)

Fallen humanity's history is the ultimate in tragic, dark comedy. In our fallen state, we are the most pathetic and stone cold stupid of all one-trick ponies that has ever defiantly pranced upon the face of God's green and previously pristine earth.

Our trick?

Rebellion.

Rebellion against God.

The God who created and sustains us.

How's that for "stone cold stupid"?

That said, exactly *how* stupid are we? How oblivious? How arrogant? How doomed?

The short answer is: Completely (see: Romans 1), apart from God's unmerited grace (see: Romans 5:8).

Our nature from birth is such that we are no more likely to notice rebellion than a fish is to notice water. We live in and breathe rebellion the same way a fish lives in and breathes water. We love sin and rebellion the way a fish loves water and wetness, which is to say *automatically* and *by nature*.

We're born this way and we like it. A lot.

That being the case, apart from God gracing us with conviction and repentance, we aren't the least little bit inclined to even notice our rebellion, much less label it as such. Until and unless He graces us with conviction and repentance, we perceive and therefore paint our rebellion in nothing but flattering, happy colors and terms because *we honestly and sincerely believe that our rebellion is good*. Cute, even. Downright awesome. Really. No joke.

As such, we are very much predisposed to refer to *our* rebellion as something reasonable and good, like "common sense". Or "empowerment". Or "being positive". Or "being nice". Or "loving". Or "kindness".. Or "good conservative (or liberal or progressive or family or libertarian) values". Or…well…you get the picture.

The bottom line is that we love to paint *our* rebellion as something so sweet and so beautiful that, quite obviously, anything opposed to it must be, by definition, bad, ugly, and probably even evil.

Here is where even in the practice and defense of our favorite stupid pony trick we accidentally confirm and, in our own warped way, agree with God's perfect perspective on such things as beauty, truth, love, justice, and every other good thing in all of His creation.

God does indeed share the perspective that there is one and only one correct standard by which to measure *all* things in *all* of His creation at *all* times, and that *all* who oppose that standard are, by definition, not only wrong, but *evil*. The trouble for humanity is that it is *entirely* born into that evil camp, and every flavor of its rebellion is evil, no matter how folksy, sweet, traditional, or intellectually appealing a label we manage to temporarily slap onto it.

Christ-dismissing liberalism?

Evil.

Christ-dismissing conservatism?

Evil.

Christ-dismissing economics?

Evil.

Christ-dismissing business practices?

Evil.

Christ-dismissing law?

Evil.

Christ-dismissing education, government, art or sexuality?

Evil, evil, evil and evil.

See the trend here? Allow me to save some time, announce the obvious, and move on: *This trend never ends.*

It has *zero* exceptions.

Never has and never will.

If we disagree with, advocate against or even cling to an apathetic view of anything that God has addressed with clarity in His perfect, *unbreakable* Word, we are, in that act, in open rebellion against Him.

We are evil.

We are a stone-cold stupid one-trick prancing pony.

The good news is that there is a cure: Repentance.

The bad news is that we cannot earn and will never choose this cure in and of our own free will, since that will is defined by our nature and, as we've already covered, our nature from birth is evil.

Only by God's grace through supernaturally inspired conviction, repentance, and restoration can the dread condition of Stone Cold Stupid Prancing Ponyitis be cured. This blessing of conviction comes through His people faithfully sharing (at great personal cost) the Gospel command to repent, believe and be saved from the coming righteous judgment of their beloved and soon returning King – the King of all creation.

The typical American response to the biblical concept of "the blessing of conviction" alone is enough to give us a good sense as to where we're at (and a good explanation as to why we are here). In a nation where the blessing of conviction is avoided like the Black Death in most churches through countless detours around and mutilations of the Gospel command to repent, believe, and be saved, it should come as no surprise that biblical truths like the "blessing of persecution" would be even more openly abhorred.

For generations now, even the most (apparently) rigorous portion of the professing Christian American subculture has been so successfully wooed by various Christ-dismissing philosophies and movements (aka "idols"), that it's hard for most professing Christians – even many true believers – to even distinguish between the tenants of these idolotrous worldviews and the Christian worldview as defined by the Word of God. In this sad context, the default for folks enamored with these idols has become to exalt the former over the latter, leading to...well... *precisely* the cultural implosion that we are witnessing now in the "Christian nation" of the United States.

Here in our land, it is the professing Christians who are, far and away, most responsible for where we are as a culture and society.

In America, professing Christendom has removed itself so far from God's Word as the authority in all realms of life that to even suggest to the typical church-going, Bible-reading, professing Christian American something like "the first goal and purpose of business is to glorify God" will almost always illicit one of three responses:

1. **Stunned silence.** This is the most hopeful of the most common responses, as it indicates at least the significant *possibility* of serious future contemplation, possibly inspired by the blessing of conviction. If conviction is not at work here, then the stunned silence is just of the typical, useless, lemming-like sort.

2. **Confused/Evasive silence.** This is where the hearer knows that the statement "just can't be true", or something like that, because it directly confronts their cherished worldview on the subject, yet they see enough to know that, at the same time, it actually must be true if Scripture is true. Their unwillingness to test their own most cherished beliefs in light of Scripture leaves them in a confused, silent stupor. These folks tend to cling to their idolatry regardless of anything Scripture has to say, but they just can't work up the honesty or courage to openly reject Scripture in word with the same clarity that they reject it in deed.

...or...

3. **Proud defiance.** This one most often sounds something like "Oh c'mon! You gotta be kidding!" ...or "Are you *nuts*?" ...or "You *are* nuts!" The bottom line here is that the defiant idolater, caught red handed, so to speak, immediately goes "all in" on the *personal* offensive approach to the conversation as a means of defending the indefensible. Usually these folks know that Scripture completely and clearly opposes their cherished worldview on the subject, so they pivot into "kill the messenger" mode. They do everything they can to destroy the credibility of the individual who has dared to shine Scriptural light onto their closely-held and adored idolatry. They can't deal with, much less embrace,

Scripture on the subject, so they vigorously avoid, dismiss and evade every relevant passage cited in context while simultaneously doing everything possible to paint the person going to Scripture for answers as the problem.

Again, we're not talkin' 'bout the "soft, lefty, phony baloney pseudo-Christians" here. We're talking about the professed (and often actually) "hard core, Bible-believing" ones who really do read their Bibles often, really do regularly attend Bible studies, and really are active members in Bible-embracing churches. These days, the purposeful application of Scripture's vivid perfection to man's political, legal, economic, and business considerations is most violently and vocally opposed by many of *these* sorts of professing Christians. Some of these Christians are true believers who are struggling against the flesh in their walk of sanctification, as we all do, and some are false converts and phony Christian-in-name-only types.

That distinction is not ours to fully grasp and is not the subject of this piece, though it should be noted that the Spirit in all true believers is such that they will embrace any credible challenge to "test their faith", where railing against such a loving, biblical challenge is one of the tell-tale signs of false conversion and phony religiosity.

What *is* respectfully introduced here for your consideration is the relationship between God's perfect Word and everything else in His creation, with "everything else" including America, Satanists, and government. It is here that we intersect with the events presently unfolding at the Oklahoma State Capitol.

As per yesterday's ABC News report, there is a tragically comedic (or comically tragic – take your pick) hubbub brewing over a Ten Commandments monument that was recently installed at the Oklahoma State Capitol and the pending arrival of a Satanic Temple equivalent in the near future.

The story reads, in part:

The privately funded Ten Commandments monument was approved by the conservative-led Oklahoma state legislature in

2009, and erected on Capitol grounds in 2012. It has riled up opponents ever since, many calling into question the constitutionality of the monument.

But [Lucien Greaves, a spokesman for the Satanic Temple] does not see a problem with the Christian monument, as long as it does not stand alone.

"I feel that the statue is only problematic when it stands alone," Greaves said. "It would change the dynamic with our monument there. We aren't objecting to the Ten Commandments monument, we're objecting to the monument standing alone."

When asked what the Satanic monument would look like, Greaves said he doesn't want to "reveal too much about the possible design options," but hinted that his "favorite design, at the moment, is an interactive display for children."

Before we take the bait and throw ourselves down any of the numerous rabbit-holes that have successfully distracted and dominated the responses of most politically inclined professing Christians (a group of which I am a member), let's make note of two very basic and very important facts that are apparent and foundational to a right and productive understanding of this story:

> 1. A group of people strongly desires that the Oklahoma State Capitol display a monument that screams open rebellion against the God of Scripture like nothing else in recent memory.

> 2. Another group wants to follow suit with a more formal monument to Satanism.

Before we flesh this out, let's consider some vital and painfully relevant biblical truths – all, Lord willing, in a Spirit of both personal humility ("There but by the grace of God go we") and boldness in defense of His name and nature (testing all things in light of Scripture and holding fast to that which is true, no matter the cost).

First off, in the truest sense, *God's perfect law is never broken*. It is pure, beautiful, and *unbreakable*(Matt 5:17-18). It is each of these things because it is a true, unblemished reflection of His very nature. It cannot be broken because He cannot be broken.

Even Satanists tend to know this at some level, as *all* people know God (Romans 1: 18-21).

All people from birth, by their very nature, love sin, hate holiness, and try to break His law at every turn. Yet in every proud, feeble attempt made, the only thing successfully broken at the end of the day is the delusional, self-worshipping, and ultimately self-destroying transgressor. When left to their own devices, people *always* choose self-rule over Christ's lordship over their life and, as a result, break themselves upon His unbreakable law. That's just what people do – it's our nature from birth, until and unless He supernaturally saves us by giving us a new nature that hates the sin we were born loving and loves the holiness we were born hating.

If we are law haters and law-breakers by nature from birth (and we are), and the law is unbreakable, leaving all who would seek its transgression only able to break themselves upon its perfect beauty and power, then it's not hard to see that, for unregenerate, unrepentant rebels against His law, things are grim.

We hate the law by nature because it convicts us of our sin (Romans 7:7), each and every manifestation of which is nothing better than proud, open rebellion against a holy God (1 John 3:4).

That last part – the bit about sin being "nothing better than proud, open rebellion against God" is well worth camping out on for a sec, if for no other reason than to ponder the fact that this truth applies to every sin in any area of life. This means that it applies even to *our* personal pet favorite sins.

It is on this point that the Oklahoma deal comes into much better focus again, if we'll only go there.

Just think of the folks who fought and paid to have that Ten Commandments monument dropped into place on the State Capitol grounds. Without trying to be or sound mean here, and really I'm not – I can relate to these folks and their concerns on many levels and I feel for them in this moment (enough to share challenging and unpopular but necessary truth, even), I cannot help but wonder and feel compelled to

57

ask: Have they even *read* the commandments on the monument that they so proudly placed in the figurative, if not literal, center of their state's public square?

If so, do they *believe* them? Do they really, actually believe that these Ten Commandments from God are the unmatched, unbreakable "gold standard" for law on earth, as dictated from God to man?

Though time does not allow us to dive deeply into the detailed composition and majesty of the Ten Commandments here (though I would encourage the reader to do just that very thing at every opportunity), let's take a moment to touch on two fundamental truths embraced as essential to the biblically defined Christian faith:

1. The Ten Commandments, like the rest of Scripture, is not a buffet line. One cannot pick and choose which of these Commands to obey, as to do so would make them a god over God and directly violate The Commandments. Such an approach to the Ten Commandments is self-refuting (and wildly popular in professing American Christendom these days).

2. The order of the Commandments is not accidental. As with everything else in His creation, His Ten Commandments to man are perfectly and purposefully arranged, making the First Commandment regarding God's nature and exclusivity the necessary prerequisite to all subsequent Commandments. Put another way, one cannot coherently make the case for the Seventh, Eighth, or Ninth Commandments without first establishing and embracing the First or Second Commandments. Put another 'nother way, **not a single one of the Commandments of God to man can be coherently or credibly removed or separated from His exclusive,** *personal* **nature**.

With these things in mind, let's have a look at the first of the Ten Commandments, upon which the rest stand and from which the rest flow:

And God spoke all these words, saying,

"I am the Lord your God, who brought you out of the land of Egypt, out of the house of slavery.

"You shall have no other gods before me."

~ Exodus 20: 1-3 ESV – bold emphasis added.)

See how clear that is?

It's really about as straightforward as it gets, isn't it?

God has commanded man to acknowledge no other gods. He has commanded man to tolerate no other gods.

That's it.

And what have we as "good Christian Americans" said in response to this crystal clear Command from God, upon which all other life-sustaining and peace-preserving Commands rest and from which they flow? We have said that **God is wrong on this one** and that anyone in *our* society run which will be run *our* way is free to join us in Christ-dismissing pride by openly, proudly worshiping any god they choose.

Your pick.

Any god, including the real One, or no god at all. Whatever. No biggie. Go for it.

Oh, and by the way, don't forget, we're a "Christian nation!" "Yay God!" and all o' that! I mean, we want His blessings, so let's at least talk big and nice about Him, right?

We are *soooooo* thankful that He has blessed America with the freedom to worship any god any way we want! How cool is that?!

Are you beginning to see and smell the wildly unbiblical problem here?

Or is your idol too important and blinding to you?

This is a question that we should honestly, eagerly, ask ourselves as we first ponder our own actual relationship to the one true God of creation – the Author of the First and all subsequent Commandments, as well as our culture's plight as it circles the drain before our very eyes.

Could it be that we have chosen, purposefully and proudly, to remove ourselves from the authority of His Word? We ought to soberly reflect on that question while remembering that to be removed from His Word is to be removed from His nature. The only reason anyone ever runs from His Word is because they are repulsed by His Word…which means that they are repulsed by His nature.

We are so far fallen and so deep in open rebellion against the God that we claim to love with our lips that we are all too willing to focus our attention and critiques on "those bad people" on the other side, practicing their own favorite forms of rebellion rather than *our* favorite forms of rebellion. We'd never put it quite that way, of course, but the reality of this situation is plain to all with eyes to see, ears to hear, and a heart to desire Scripture and conform to its perfection.

Talking about "those people" who are "wrecking the country" is our favorite pastime. It's our sport. It's our favorite soap opera; our preferred form of entertainment, standing head and shoulders above everything else. Like an idol, you might say.

"Those Satanists" and "those liberals" and "those progressives" and "that Barack Obama" are not to be the first and main problem here, folks.

We are.

We are the ones called to repent, seek His will, and submit to it in order to save our land.

In this context, let us consider another in the long line of favorite, oft-quoted, yet rarely-embraced and applied passages:

> *. . . if __my people__ who are called by my name humble themselves, and pray and seek my face and turn from their wicked ways, then I will hear from heaven and will forgive their sin and heal their land.*

~ 2 Chronicles 7:14 (emphasis added)

This one's so familiar and so oft-recited that you may have seen it on a greeting card or a tee shirt and very probably in a Facebook post or Twitter feed.

But like so much else in America, the beautiful truth of this unbreakable promise has been morphed into a magic ticket to seek and

60

gain the favor of a God before whom we will not humble ourselves. We will not repent. We will not obey.

And He better just deal with it and give us what we want!

It is here that we must be reminded of the fact that God doesn't need America. Not one little bit.

He doesn't need you. He doesn't need me.

He is God. He needs nothing, including America.

Moreover, everything in all of His creation – once again, including America – *will* glorify Him. It will glorify Him through the validation of His nature as reflected in His Law. It will do so either by submitting to His Law and finding the true peace, joy, and prosperity that can only come through such an approach, or it will validate the *unbreakable* beauty, truth, and power of His Law by breaking itself upon that Law in unrepentant rebellion. Either way, God will be perfectly glorified.

So get over yourself.

And get over America.

Pride easily defines and dooms both individuals and cultures, but for the intervening grace of God inspiring conviction, repentance, and restoration.

"If my people who are called by my name humble themselves..."

Well, will they? In America?

That is my hope and prayer.

The only way to save or heal the land is for His people who are in that land to personally seek and submit to His perfect nature as revealed in His perfect Word.

An America founded on the core principle of the freedom to worship any and all gods is an America that must repent or she will be justly and properly crushed under the weight of her rebellion.

An America in open embrace with explicitly unbiblical practices such as en economic matrix built upon fiat currency (which, through its abandonment of biblical standards, enslaves *by design*) and the "freedom to choose" not only the worship of any old god, but the murder of innocent children *for convenience,* is an America that must repent or be destroyed as a consequence of her freely chosen and proudly adored rebellion.

This is where we are and who we are.

We are rebels against God.

That understood, why wouldn't we expect and tolerate a Satanic Temple monument next to our proudly placed but never read/applied monument to the Ten *Commandments*?

Why?

What could possibly surprise us about this?

The irony and humor factor is not hard to find here either, tragic and dark though the stage upon which it dances may be.

We claim to be a "Christian nation" yet we are all about *pride* in an America that centers its idolotrous (per)version of "freedom" on the "right" to worship any god one chooses…in direct and open rejection of the First Commandment to man from the God we claim to love! We even thank Him for giving us such "rights". Really!

While He has given us no such "right", He has certainly given us the freedom to repent or rebel, and as with any other person or culture, when left to our own devices (aka "pride"), we have and will always choose rebellion and death. At this moment in our history, our unique claim to fame is that, when it comes to sheer size and scale of blasphemy and idolatry, there has never in all of human history been a greater, more boastful spiritual whore than America. There's not even a close second, really, though one could make the case for Old Testament Israel being the closest thing to a competitor for this particular award.

What makes America truly untouchable in this contest isn't just the globe-spanning scope and influence of her rank prostitution. It's the fact that she does it all while mouthing her "love for Jesus" that makes it a truly unique and bone chilling horror. This combo allows her to coast to the easiest of wins where the gold medal for rebellion is concerned.

But hey, if you're gonna do something, be the best at that thing, right?

And in America, if there's one thing we know, it's that we're #1!

U! S! A!

U! S! A!

U! S! A!

We actually refer to ourselves as "the shining city on the hill". Yeah, really!

Nobody – but *nobody* – does rebellion quite like us.

The tragic comedy that is even now unfolding in Oklahoma gives us a clear and painful glimpse of this truth.

God uses all of His creation to demonstrate the perfection of His Law, even "Satanists"...in this instance, to call (and reveal) the bluff of ignorant (at best) "conservative Christians" who like to use things like the Ten Commandments as props while, in practice, utterly rejecting them as the basis for actual law.

You see, **both** groups are mocking God.

And He will not be mocked.

This reality is presently grinding up the "conservative Christians" in question and will get to the "Satanists" in due time. That is not in question.

That said, what is most sad to observe at this moment is not the temporary apparent victory of those crazy-bad, evil-liberal "Satanists" in America, but the clear, present, and *very* proud rebellion of those claiming to carry the banner of Christ in the culture war as it rages in the middle of America's blasphemously mislabeled "Bible belt".

Maybe if the self-professed "conservative Christian" folks in question would actually *read* the words – crystal clear commands (not to be confused with "suggestions") from God to man – and actually...[gasp]...**obeyed** them when they went about the business of, oh, I dunno...**legislating** or **shaping policy**, then the Ten Commandment-bearing plaques, posters and monuments littering this rapidly decomposing shipwreck of a republic would look and smell less like the toothless, Christ-mocking props that they so clearly are today.

Maybe, just maybe, by God's grace, these plaques, posters, and monuments would, for the first time, become cherished symbols to an obedient people who, out of love and honor for the one true God, would boldly oppose and cast down the "many gods" of pluralism. Maybe they would become a people inspired by the Lord of creation to repent of their worship of the "founding fathers" and Constitution as gold standards for

63

lawmakers and law. Maybe through that repentance they would be graced with a restored, loving relationship with the one and only true King, who is the one and only Source of true peace- and life-preserving law. Maybe then their land would be healed, as it can only be, on His terms according to His Word.

'Til then, score another one for God and against 'Merica...by way of His property, the Bible Belt Satanists (both sets).

3

SECTION THREE

The Consequences of Satanic "Religious Liberty"

"RELIGIOUS LIBERTY" FOR ALL
MUSLIMS
WITCHES
AND
SATANISTS
IN
AMERICA
ISN'T GOING TO SAVE US
IT'S GOING TO KILL US

Fox News Equates God's Law With Islam. American "Conservative Christians" say, "Amen!"

(Originally published at *Fire Breathing Christian* on September 9, 2015.)

If there's one thing that *absolutely terrifies* the typical politically "conservative" churchgoing professing Christian in America, it is the Nature of God as revealed in His Word and Law.

More specifically, they're petrified at even the thought of that Law-Word being taken *seriously*.

As in: *applied*.

As in: *for real*.

As in: Not just out there "in Heaven" or in some future world to come or neatly sequestered in our churches or in our prayer closets or in our precious little hearts, but...[*gasp!*]...*right here* and *right now*.

You know, like in the Great Commission:

> And Jesus came and said to them, "**<u>All</u> authority in heaven and <u>on earth</u> has been given to me.** Go therefore and make **<u>disciples</u> of all nations**, baptizing them in the name of the Father and of the Son and of the Holy Spirit, **teaching them to obey <u>all</u> that I have commanded you**. And behold, I am with you always, to the end of the age."

~ Jesus (the real One), in Matthew 28:18-20 (emphasis added)

Why is this so?

Why do most professing Christians – including most self-described "conservatives" – so *hate* the Nature of God as revealed in His Law?

Well, there are many reasons, but two biggies are:

1. **Many of them are false converts.** They hate the thought of having Christ to rule over them in every area of life because they have not been supernaturally saved by the grace of God and

transformed into obedient disciples. They may (and often do) regularly attend church, vote very "conservatively", sing in church choirs and appear to be the nicest, most polite, and well-groomed goats you ever did see, but they are goats nonetheless. As such, they will not have Christ to rule over them and even the suggestion of Him *actually*, *really*, and *truly* ruling over them *in detail* gives them the creeps and makes 'em squirm inside.

2. **Many of them are misled by unbelieving "pastors" and "priests".** Where "back in the day" American pulpits were *loaded* with pastors who were thoroughly Calvinistic and explicitly *optimistic* about the real-world life- and culture-transforming power of the Gospel-fueled Great Commission, these days even the vast majority of "church leaders" in self-described conservative, Bible-based churches have and therefore promote no appetite for the supernatural Gospel and Great Commission of Jesus Christ.

The bottom line at the end of the day is *unbelief* – unbelief in the Word of God as the *actual* standard for truth in *all* things in His creation, which then naturally produces unbelief *in practice* when it comes to specific areas of life like law, civil government, economics, and children's education.

Over the past several generations, the professing Christian church has led American culture in its abandonment of God's Word as authoritative in all areas of life. It is this false-Christianity-shaped landscape in which secular/pagan "conservative" American Statism has become the default religion of most "conservative Christians" in the land.

This is why most American "conservative Christians" are now conditioned to actually *approve* of comparisons of the Word of God with the satanic false religion of Islam as a means by which the Word of God might be discredited as the standard by which we ought to actually approach law and civil government here in this part of His creation.

It's incredible when you stop to notice and think of it.

Painful, too.

But there it is.

American professing Christians now *openly and boldly proclaim and defend* the necessity of going somewhere *other than the Word of God* for our understanding, pursuit, and application of law and civil government.

"Christians" do this!

All the time in America.

Which is why Fox News can now routinely do ***this*** (as reported today by World Net Daily, with emphasis added):

> Shepard Smith, Fox News host, cut into his own press conference coverage of the release of Kentucky clerk Kim Davis from jail to **rail against her**, as well as those who supported her denial of wedding certificates to same-sex couples, saying such is simply **a "religious play" that has no business in government service**.
>
> **He also compared Kim Davis supporters to those who oppose Sharia law**, characterizing them as one and the same when it comes to ideology.
>
> "They set this up as a religious play again," Smith said, Mediaite reported. **"This is the same crowd that says, 'We don't want Sharia law,' don't let them tell us what to do, keep their religion out of our lives and out of our government.' Well, here we go again."**

Remember: Everyone is theocratic.

You're theocratic. I'm theocratic. Shepard Smith is theocratic.

Everyone is theocratic in that we all want the laws of *our* god to be obeyed. We have each chosen our source for law. That chosen source is our god *in practice*.

Generally speaking for the unconverted, the choice of god they prefer is *themselves*. This is why unsaved masses of people very much like the idea of "We the People" as god *in practice*. That pitch works very well on the proud and the lost, particularly when used as the tool of a particular overarching religious worldview known as *Statism*.

This is why Fox News – a wholly owned tool and advocate of Statism – is actively opposed to *any* religion that would dare place itself above the State. This is why Fox News and its most well-programmed followers vigorously attack *any* religion that would dare compete with *their* religion, in which the Almighty (American) State is god *in practice*.

After years and decades and generations of Statist programming, we are now a land loaded with professing Christians who absolutely eat up the blasphemous comparison of God's Law to Islamic law for the sake of discrediting both as inferior and dangerous to the One True Law of the Almighty American State.

This is why we hear all sorts of nonsense now regularly flowing from supposedly "conservative Christian" minds and mouths in America. Things like:

- "Um, uh, if we don't want Sharia Law then we can't want biblical law, right?"

- "I mean, this is America! We are "free" here to worship any god we like, and the only way we can really do that is to not submit to any particular one of 'em, right?"

  ...and...my *favorite*...

- "But if we advocate God's Law while resisting Muslim application of Islamic Law, aren't we being hypocritical? Aren't we being just like them? What's the difference between us advocating for our God's law and them advocating for theirs?"

What's the difference?
What's the difference?!
Well howsabout *this*, my **professing conservative Christian** friend:

Islam is a <u>false</u> religion proclaiming a <u>false</u> gospel and a <u>false</u> god, and <u>Jesus Christ is the one true God</u> who has lovingly <u>commanded</u> and <u>equipped</u> us to become and propagate <u>disciples</u> who actively

70

strive to learn and <u>obey all that He has commanded!</u> (See: ~~Pretty much~~ your whole Bible.)

Hello?!

What do I need here, ginormous neon letters?

Maybe some giant burning flags waving next to that paragraph?

I mean, what...do...you...*need*, "Christian", to see the most basic of realities here:

Our God *is* God.

Theirs is *not*.

Get it?

See the significance here?

Their god is a satanic counterfeit.

Just like Fox News' god and gospel of All-American "conservative" *Statism*.

And *our* God – the real one, remember? – **has commanded and equipped His people to faithfully proclaim and apply His Nature as revealed in His Word in each and every realm of His creation and area of our lives.**

Which *includes* law, politics, and civil government.

In America.

Right now.

No matter what Fox "News" tells you.

Detroit celebrates All-American "right" to worship Satan. [insert "U! S! A!" chant here]

(Originally published at *Fire Breathing Christian* on July 25, 2015.)

For all o' those professing conservative Christians in America who are somehow actually still confused as to "how, oh how(!)" our culture could have possibly sunk so quickly and deeply into its present vile and disgusting state, our friends the Satanists have once again come along on cue to dutifully remind us of what is *really* at the root of all the multigenerational cultural rot that's now coming into full bloom here in "the land of the free" and the home of the NSA.

Yes, even Satanists are ultimately God's tools, whether they like it or not (and they don't).

So how is God using these sad, deranged little advocates of suicidal pride in America these days?

Well, there are many ways, of course, but the one we'll take a sec to focus on here is the manner in which He's using them to demonstrate – in increasingly flagrant fashion – the suicidally stupid and destructive power of our All-American adoration of religious pluralism.

Put another way, God is using these particular tools at this particular time to demonstrate once again that His Word is not optional. It is binding…right here and right now…even in America.

So when CBS reports, as they did today, that Detroit is set to host "the largest public satanic ceremony in history" at which a giant statue of Satan will be proudly unveiled and worshipped under the protection of American-style counterfeit "freedom" and "liberty", we really shouldn't be surprised.

At all.

This is just "the right to freely worship any god you want" in action.

And what could be more American than that?

So the next time you hear someone – especially a professing conservative Christian – in America act all confused and appalled at the way the Big Gay Wave is rolling over the culture or how child sacrifice is an openly ongoing and "legally" protected business in America, kindly ask them what they think of the All-American approach to "rights" – particularly the so-called "God-given 'right' to worship any god".

Ask them what the ruling Law of the land really is?

Ask them if they really believe that America has the power to make "legal" that which God has declared to be lawless?

Get them to thinking…lovingly, graciously, but firmly.

That's what we need here and now in America. More than ever before.

Until we lovingly *confront* and *correct* this culture – beginning in the professing Christian sub-culture – with the Gospel-fueled Great Commission, we are doomed to a future of more and more murdered babies, the normalization of more and more sexual perversion, and the open worship of more and more satanic false gods…all pursued *proudly* in the name of American-style "freedom" and "liberty".

Religious "Freedom" Update: Witch leads American heartland "lawmakers" in "prayer".

(Originally published at *Fire Breathing Christian* on April 10, 2015.)

So how's that "right" to worship any god treating you, America?

How's it goin' in the land of the free to worship and pray openly to any ol' god (or goddess) that happens to impress you at any given moment?

Well, if Iowa is any indicator, things are going pretty much *exactly* as Scripture warns (see: Romans 1). We have been given over under the unfolding wrath of God. We are blind, deaf, and stone-hearted to His truth. We are also both proud and confident.

Why?

'Cause we're Americans!

And while it's nearly impossible to keep up with the hourly examples of God's judgment upon us, nowhere has our insanity been more perfectly summarized this week than in the Iowa State Legislature, where, in the name of – what else? – good ol' American religious pluralism, a wiccan was invited to deliver the invocation at the State House of Representative's opening ceremony.

In *'Blessed Be, Aho, and Amen,' Wiccan Priestess Delivers Prayer for Iowa House*, linked through the Drudge Report this week, we are treated to the following tale of religious pluralism gone wild, happy, and free in the heartland of America:

> *"Blessed Be, Aho, and Amen," aren't the words members of the Iowa House of Representatives are accustomed to hear at the closing of the invocation marking the House's opening ceremonies, but that's just what happened yesterday when a Wiccan priestess delivered the prayer.*
>
> *"We call this morning to God, Goddess, Universe, that which is greater than ourselves to be here with us today," said Deborah*

Maynard, who delivered the first prayer by a Wiccan in the assembly. "By the Earth that is in our bones and centers us, may all here remember our roots and those whom we are here to represent..... We call this morning to Spirit, which is ever present, to help us respect the interdependent web of all existence of which we are a part. Be with this legislative body and guide them to seek justice, equity and compassion in the work that is before them today."

But don't worry. Some Christians noticed and "took action"!
The story continues:

A number of Christian lawmakers didn't attend the opening ceremony to protest the priestess' historic invocation.

Others, like State Rep. Rob Taylor (R-Iowa), turned their backs during the priestess' prayer. Taylor said he asked himself "What would Jesus do?" and decided Jesus would "be in the presence of a prayer, but peacefully protest." He added that "everyone has the right to come into our chamber – it is the people's chamber – and pray and she did and this was the way for me to peacefully protest."

Let's focus on that last sentence, 'cause it's a doozy...and *very* important:
". . .everyone has the right to come into our chamber – it is the people's chamber – and pray and she did and this was the way for me to peacefully protest."

This, my fellow Americans, is what it looks like when the authority of God is replaced with the authority of "we the people".
This is what it looks like when people who are at best biblically illiterate and at worst overtly anti-Christian are placed by God into positions of leadership.

This is the rebellion of religious pluralism in action, and wicked leadership is but one of the many consequences that we are reaping through that rebellion.

This is what freedom, liberty, and justice look like when severed from the Nature of God as revealed in His Word.

May God grace His people with the strength, opportunity, and fortitude to stand upon, proclaim, and apply His Nature as revealed in His Word right here and now in this dark hour…while there is yet time.

Why Gays Love (and Laugh at) Christian Appeals to "Religious Tolerance"

(Originally published at *Fire Breathing Christian* on April 28, 2015.)

One by one, lessons as to how things actually work in the real world are piling up. (And by "the real world", I mean the *real* one…as in: owned, operated, and defined by God.)

One by one, the casualty list is growing (and usually at a pace that makes single casualties' distinctions blur).

One by one, thresholds are reached and then breached. Unthinkable new lows are reached and then quickly become normative on the way down to the next "unthinkable" new low (and soon to be new norm).

One by one, the lies we've been pitched, sold and enthusiastically embraced as truth are being revealed to be nothing better than the most vile and corrosive of lies.

This is what happens when cultures buy into the serpent's spin on how things work in "the real world".

Nowhere have the consequences of Christians buying into the serpent's take on "real world" living been more apparent than in the ongoing hot-knife-through-butter campaign of the LGBT(QRSTUV…) movement. While the forces of secular "progress" and enforced pagan tolerance seem to understand that *they cannot tolerate* the continued presence and influence of obedient Christians in the culture, their efforts to persecute Christians into silence has been most greatly aided by professing Christians themselves who have compliantly provided the "hot butter" through which the knife of Secularism now cuts with little, if any, meaningful resistance.

Most Christians aiming to defend the owners of the Sweet Cakes bakery, who were forced out of business for refusing to create a "gay wedding" cake and are still being hounded relentlessly by The Forces of Tolerance, are even now relying on secular pragmatic arguments that often directly contradict the Word of God as the standard by which we all must live.

In a recent article posted at Fox News, we learn that "Big Christian" names in the middle of the battle are still clinging to religious pluralism as a *virtue* that will somehow, some way, save the day for biblically obedient Christians. This bizarre turning of biblical truth on its head may be painful to witness and tiresome to contemplate again and again as it repeats its failed arguments and approaches for the zillionth time (what was it that Einstein said about that sort of thing?), but we are well served to do just that. If we love all of those involved in this battle, and we seek to honor the Lord in an effective manner on the battlefield in which we've been purposefully placed, then we must point out at every critical opportunity that standing on anything other than the Word of God as our basis for life in the real world –*His* real world – can, will, and should ultimately lead to ever increasing darkness and ultimately death.

To put a finer point on it: Claiming Christianity while standing for the "virtue" of religious pluralism is never, ever, **ever** gonna get us anywhere good. **God despises religious pluralism** as it is now championed by America-first "Christians", and we must repent of that view before true cultural resurrection can be achieved.

As for the ongoing pragmatic/pluralistic defenses of Aaron and Melissa Klein (of Sweet Cakes by Melissa fame), Todd Starnes recently wrote for *Fox News* that:

> *Franklin Graham has announced he will back a fundraising effort to help Aaron and Melissa Klein, the owners of Sweet Cakes By Melissa in Oregon.*
>
> *"We're all in real danger if something isn't done to put a stop to this kind of deliberate targeting and malicious treatment of Christians," Graham wrote on his Facebook page.*
>
> *On Friday a judge for the Oregon Bureau of Labor and Industries (BOLI) recommended a lesbian couple should receive $135,000 in damages for their emotional suffering after the Kleins refused to make them a wedding cake.*
>
> *The Kleins have already lost their home. Now the government and the LGBT activists want to throw them out on the street.*

The article continued to chronicle some significant twists and details:

Within hours of the ruling, the Family Research Council facilitated the establishment of a GoFundMe account to help the Christian family raise the money they needed to pay the fine. In less than eight hours, more than $100,000 was raised.

However, late Friday GoFundMe pulled the plug — sending this message to would-be donors:

"After careful review by our team, we have found the 'Support Sweet Cakes By Melissa' campaign to be in violation of our Terms and Conditions," the message read. "The money raised thus far will still be made available for withdrawal."

Family Research Council president Tony Perkins said GoFundMe caved under pressure from gay activists.

Enter Franklin Graham.

He decided to let people donate to the Klein family through Samaritan's Purse.

"The Kleins have already had to close their Oregon bakery business, Sweet Cakes by Melissa and do not have this money to pay," Graham wrote. "Aaron said it would financially ruin their family and could cost them their home. They have done nothing wrong, and their lives, along with their five children, have been turned upside down by this persecution."

Graham doubled down on his assertion that what is happening to the family is persecution.

"You can't call it anything else," he wrote. "This is wrong, and it's happening right here in our own country. Liberal judges and officials siding with the LGBT crowd are trying to make a point with the undeserved punishment of this family. This is America— we should have the freedom to live by our sincerely held religious beliefs. It's obvious who is really being discriminated against here."

Notice that last line: "This is America—we should have the freedom to live by our sincerely held religious beliefs."

Now ask yourself this: Did Franklin Graham (and those parroting the same by-now-obviously-ineffective "defense") get that argument from Scripture or from somewhere else…like maybe secular American tradition? In order to believe that this same freedom extends to, say, Muslims in America, is there any way to reconcile this veneration of (and subsequent dependence upon) religious pluralism with the Nature of the one true God as revealed in His Word?

Nope.

And we all know it.

Yet we keep right on appealing to the idol of religious pluralism so that it might provide our salvation, when the God that we claim with our lips clearly and lovingly demands that we take a completely different path.

The fact that God *despises* the sort of religious pluralism that the likes of Graham constantly appeal to as a defense for beleaguered Christians ought to tell us something. Many somethings, actually. Perhaps chief among them being that we just might be bringing the judgment of God down upon these Christian-run businesses by our constant appeals to things like All-American religious pluralism, which stand in direct contradiction to the crystal clear Word of God.

So, in effect, it seems quite likely that, once again, professing Christians in America are most responsible for bringing about their own persecution and the ongoing darkening of the culture.

All of this is happening because we as professing Christians have bought into the foundational lie that God is personally non-essential when it comes to cultural or civilizational life in detail.

The Deadly Myth of Neutrality

One of the most popular and assumed-to-be-true lies that has come to define our culture is the *myth of neutrality* – the idea that anyone (or any group or any government) can take a position that is neutral with regard to any aspect of God's Nature as clearly revealed in His Word.

The world tells us that it is not only possible, but *necessary* for men, women, groups and governments to take "neutral" positions on any number of clear pronouncements from God where those pronouncements challenge or conflict with the accepted and often cherished norms here in "the real world" – a "real world" that, we are told, isn't actually under the rule of God in any kind of detailed, comprehensive manner.

This myth of neutrality is an echo from Eden that is so utterly appealing to our sinful, selfish nature that, apart from the saving grace of God, we find it irresistible. Our inherent desire to judge God, test God, correct God, reject God, and ultimately replace God (with ourselves) in practice is irrepressible apart from the supernatural intervention of God in our lives, raising us from spiritual death unto life and inspiring us to broken repentance over our sin so that we might then, all by His grace, begin to pursue the holiness that we once hated while resisting the sin that we once adored.

Once again in the case of Sweet Cakes by Melissa, our only true hope lies in the Nature of God as revealed in His perfect, sufficient Word. Once again, the Gospel-fueled Great Commission is our only legitimate response to every argument from any angle in this episode of the ongoing culture war in America.

Appeals to the things that God hates – like religious pluralism – cannot save us.

Submitting to the Forces of Tolerance and surrendering yet another hill on the cultural battlefield will not save us.

Appealing to God's Nature as revealed in His Word and submitting to Christ as King in practice is our only hope. It is all that we need. And infinitely more.

Lord willing, His people will realize this while there is yet time so that they might drop the plastic weapons that our enemies insist we use and take up instead the Sword of Truth and the Gospel-fueled Great Commission, by which every enemy can and will be conquered, by His grace, for His glory, and to our eternal benefit.

Senate candidate admits to sacrificing a goat and drinking its blood.

(Originally published at *Fire Breathing Christian* on October 7, 2015.)

So what if somebody wants to drink a little goat blood as part of their pursuit of religious liberty in America?

I mean, isn't that what we're all about?

"Religious liberty", I mean.

As in, the "God-given right" to openly worship false gods, including the devil himself.

(See how utterly *insane* that is when you simply clarify the concept in print that way?)

As AP reported earlier this week:

> "Two years ago, Augustus Sol Invictus walked from central Florida to the Mojave Desert and spent a week fasting and praying, at times thinking he wouldn't survive. In a pagan ritual to give thanks when he returned home, he killed a goat and drank its blood.
>
> Now that he's a candidate for U.S. Senate, the story is coming back to bite him."

While it's nice to see that news of Mr. Invictus' goat sacrificing background isn't exactly helping his campaign, let's be perfectly clear about one thing: **The modern American Statist construct of "religious liberty" not only allows for but vigorously protects open pagan worship.** While there may be certain laws in place (for now; "law" based on the will of man is a constantly shifting thing) protecting goats and other animals from certain treatment, when it comes to the open worship of false gods, including the devil himself, Americans – including most professing Christian Americans – have been conditioned to champion such behavior as – *get this* – a "God-given right".

While Mr. Invictus is quite unlikely to win any state-level elections any time soon, the longer we persist in our anti-Christian approach to "religious liberty", the more openly Pagan-friendly (and Christianity-hating) the voting populace will become. This is the wrath of God upon us. This is the consequence of our proud, All-American repudiation of the crystal clear Nature of God as revealed in His Word.

As we covered last month in *Should Muslims and Satanists be allowed to seek public office in America?*:

> God is explaining to us that in His creation the open worship of false Gods is always destructive. It always leads to death. There are no exceptions. Thus, out of love for us, He gives us life-preserving clarity on the matter in His Word.
>
> So when we ditch His Word and grab on to the notion of secular "religious pluralism" as a good and noble thing, we are both mocking God and begging for His wrath upon our land and culture. When we embrace the idea that "We the People" are free to openly worship any god we like and that this is a great virtue that not only serves as a central pillar of our culture, but is also something that all other cultures in the world ought to be encouraged to emulate, we are both mocking God and begging for His wrath upon our land and culture…and the lands and cultures that follow our lead.
>
> When we embrace *that* explicitly *anti*-Christian concept of "religious liberty" and hold it high, we are begging for our own destruction.
>
> Potential Muslim or Satanist or [insert any particular anti-Christ religious category here] candidate-for-President questions are symptomatic. The fact that they are almost always asked in a context that *presumes* the legality of openly practicing Muslims or Satanists or whatever in America demonstrates that we have a far more profound and far more foundational problem on our hands…and we don't even know it.
>
> The question that we *should* be asking – but are discouraged at every turn from even noticing, much less contemplating – is the

question as to the true legality of the open worship of false gods in the first place. As in: What has God said about this? What has God said is legally allowed in His creation where the worship of false gods is concerned? What has He commanded in this regard? And what has He promised will result from rejection of His life-giving Word on the subject?

Put another way, will we now seek, repent, and submit to the crystal clear Word of God on this vital question?

Or will "We the People" continue to cling to our pride and rebellion, even as our America Idol disintegrates into chaos all around us?

Will we keep symptomatically chattering on and on about the symptoms of the symptoms of the symptoms of our fundamental rejection of the lordship of Christ?

Or will we cut to the chase, take the axe to the root, finally repent and submit to Christ as King *in practice*?

May God grace us with broken, humble repentance, submission, and the otherwise impossible restoration to follow…while there is yet time.

"If you love me, you will keep my commandments."

~ Jesus (the real One), in John 14:15

We've been allowing these Pagan Right Wing Statists to educate, manipulate, and use us for generations now. It's well past time that we stop supporting them and start actively opposing them.

It's time that we stop feeding our children to them for "education".

They really do adore and will always encourage us (and our children) to embrace the God-hated concept of religious pluralism. They really and truly believe that all "lesser gods" ought to be freely worshipped as a sort of placebo for the masses, so long as said masses understand clearly that the true God above all others *in practice* is the Almighty State.

In this America is not different from Rome at its core. The State is god in practice, and anyone who will not acknowledge this and submit accordingly must – and *will* – be punished.

See: Kim Davis.

If we want to actually deal with the problem of **Islam** in America, we will have to reject the "religious liberty" approach of our Pagan Political "leaders" and experts.

If we want to successfully address the problem of Witchcraft and Satanism in America, we will have to repent of our enabling them through this satanic construct of "religious liberty" and submit to the loving rule of Christ as King in practice.

If we don't want witches leading our "legislators" in "prayer" anymore in America, we have to repent and submit to the God we've mocked through our perverse approach to "religious liberty".

See again how profoundly un-American all of that sounds these days?

Stop witchcraft?!

Outlaw Islam?!

Ban Satanism?!

Sounds pretty crazy in our proud All-American modern context, doesn't it?

Of course it does.

And that should tell us all we need to know about America and where she stands in the eyes of the one true God…who will *not* be mocked by *any* nation…'Merica included (see: Psalm 2).

May He grace us with repentance and restoration while there is yet time.

This Satanic Temple Holiday Display Has Been Brought To You By: American Pride and "Freedom"

(Originally published at *Fire Breathing Christian* on December 4, 2014.)

So what does it look like for a culture to proudly, arrogantly, and openly mock God?

Well, just check out this headline from CBS:

Satanic Temple Approved For Capitol Holiday Display

And what culture would dare to openly mock the God of creation in such a flagrant and vile manner?

Why 'Merica, of course.

[insert "*U! S! A!*" chant here]

The article was published today right here in our oh so proud land of "freedom" – including, of course, the freedom to openly worship any false god in direct violation of all o' those Ten Commandments plaques that professing Christians in America fight to have on display everywhere but never seem to actually read, much less obey.

In the CBS piece, we are informed that, "Florida's Capitol will have a new holiday decoration this year. The Satanic Temple will be among its nativity scenes and secular presentations."

How sweet.

How tolerant.

How very *American.*

…and how perfectly ironic that the persistently *ignored* text on all of those Ten Commandments plaques is the very thing that would have lovingly prevented anything resembling a Satanic Temple display from finding its way to open public display and…*ahem*…*worship.*

The post goes on:

Lucien Greaves, spokesman for the Satanic Temple, said in an email that "the difference seems to be in the fact that this time around we arrived with lawyers."

The temple, which threatened to sue after being rejected last year but never took action, is scheduled to put up its display Dec. 22.

The approved display will banner the phrase "Happy holidays from the Satanic Temple" atop a diorama of an angel falling into hell.

"We hope that, this holiday season, everybody can put their religious differences aside and respect that the celebratory spirit of responsible hedonism is available to all," Greaves said in the email.

And there we have it.

Again.

What "it", you ask?

Why, the judgment of God, of course. It's on full display here. *Again.* God has spoken with clarity: We shall not allow for the open worship of false Gods. At all. Ever. Period.

And what is America's ever-so *proud* response?

Something like: "Thank you, and boy, do we ever respect you and like you and all, but we just disagree on this one. We know you'll understand since you're such a nice, good, gracious and forgiving God and all…"

Or: "Look, we like *some* of your commandments and are fine with putting *them* into *our* law, but this one at the top, um…*not so much*…"

Or: "Nope."

So you can see the problem.

We have – from the very beginning – taken the first and most important of the Ten Commandments and overturned it entirely as though we could somehow skip the defense of His exclusive name and nature entirely and move on to the other, more pragmatic and appealing commandments. In typical man-centered fashion, we wanted the benefits of God without God Himself. And we put it in *writing*…writing that we now worship here in America.

Can idolatry get any more rank and obvious than this?

Hardly.

Yet we seem to be so very blind to it here in America.

Why?

What has prevented us from noticing this raging, glaring mockery of God's nature as revealed in His Law and inscribed on all those tablets and plaques that hypocritical evangelicals fight tooth and nail to have scattered around government grounds and State-controlled children's "education" facilities dedicated to immersing our children in the satanic approach to the pursuit of knowledge? (See: Genesis 3.)

The answer to that one is simple.

Painful, but simple.

It's *pride*.

Good ol' American pride.

And that "good ol' American pride" along with its now multi-generational unbiblical traditions have become the religion *in practice* of even most professing Christians in America.

So, once again, it is the professing Christian church that is *most* responsible for the culture's embrace of Socialism in practice. Even most American professing Christians will defend the preservation of rank Marxist/Socialist systems like Social Security and Public Schools...all while amazingly considering themselves to be "conservative", to boot.

The main reason for that, of course, is because most of those automatic defenders of Socialism and Statism were themselves trained by the State in, you guessed it, public "schools".

See how that works?

See how we got here?

See where dismissing the Word and Law of God has taken us?

It all began with the rejection of our personal, real world, right now obligation to actively defend the exclusivity of God as the *personal* source of *all* true, lasting liberty and freedom.

From there it has led, as of this moment, to the open presentation of Satanic Temple holiday displays on government grounds.

And it will only get worse – *much worse* – from here...*until and unless we repent and submit to Christ the King.*

See?

It's not tricky at all, really, now is it?

Yeah, as we mentioned earlier, it's definitely *painful*, but not hard to see at all.

So will this proud America repent and submit to the King of Kings?

Or will it be broken under the weight of His inescapable, unbreakable Word?

The answer to these vital questions, Christian, is first up to *us*. If, by God's grace, we openly, clearly repent of *our* rebellion and support of rebellion, however "patriotic" or "traditionally American" that rebellion may have been, then – *and only then* – there is hope.

Only then can we credibly take up the Gospel-fueled Great Commission to make disciples who will do *all* that Christ the King has commanded (see: Matthew 28). Then we can and will see even this most dark and dying of cultures miraculously resurrected…one supernatural salvation at a time.

So let's get to tearing down enemy strongholds and bringing *every* thought captive to Christ our King (2 Corinthians 10:4-5)…beginning right here and now with our personal commitment to repudiate the notion of a "right" to worship false gods and taking up our *personal obligation* to defend His exclusive nature as the explicit, essential source of all true freedom, liberty, peace, and prosperity.

Soli Deo Gloria…and let's roll!

Well color me satanic and call me America! (Or: How our cherished tolerance for false gods is killing us.)

(Originally published at *Fire Breathing Christian* on September 22, 2014.)

While there are many profound problems with the notion of religious pluralism as enshrined in American culture, the biggest bad thing about our wildly unbiblical permissive approach to life and worship is that God despises it.

In a tragic yet anything-but-surprising alert posted by the good folks at *Stand Up for the Truth* this morning, we learn of the latest in a *looooong* line of explicitly satanic advances planned and soon-to-be accomplished through the coherent, legitimate use of the American idol of religious pluralism as captured and celebrated in the First Amendment to the United States Constitution:

> *While both the Freedom From Religion Foundation, a secular activist group, and The Satanic Temple, a New York City-based organization that "facilitates the communication and mobilization of politically aware Satanists," disagree with the decision to allow religious materials, both plan to combat Bible dissemination by giving out their own ideological literature at public schools in Orange County.*

Just what sort of literature are the good (or is that evil?) folks at The Satanic Temple planning on distributing to children in State-controlled "schools"?

Howsabout satanic coloring books?

America's Proud Commitment to the Worship of False Gods

Yes, my fellow Americans, this is where tossing the Nature of God as revealed in His Word as our standard has gotten us. This is how far we've fallen...for now (it'll soon get much, much worse)...

> *"If a public school board is going to allow religious pamphlets and full Bibles to be distributed to students ... we think the responsible thing to do is to ensure that these students are given access to a variety of differing religious opinions," Satanic Temple spokesman Lucien Greaves said in a statement. "As opposed to standing idly by while one religious voice dominates the discourse and delivers propaganda to youth." Among the literature that the Satanist organization reportedly plans to deliver to kids is "The Satanic Children's Big Book of Activities," a coloring book that focuses on Satanic themes and human tolerance.*

And why not? If America is all about the freedom to worship *any* god, then what is there to stop these things from continuing, growing, and metastasizing?

Come to think of it, what has there *ever* been to pevent such openly satanic proliferation?

When "We the people" so long ago traded in God for the Founding Fathers as the gold standard in Law Giver and the Bible for the Constitution as the gold standard in law, were we not at that moment doomed to reach this point...and worse?

Has God not spoken with sufficient clarity as to His detestation of allowing false gods to be worshipped in the land?

How surprised can we truly be at what is now happening in this land as a result of our open, willful, and oh-so-*proud* rebellion against the clarity of His Word?

Just some food for thought there, Christian...

Lord willing, He will inspire true conviction, repentance, and restoration in His people...while there is yet time...and ideally *before* we get to see what comes after satanic coloring books....

The homo-jihad's continuing "education" of the infidels.

(Originally published at *Fire Breathing Christian* on April 9, 2015.)

Blood is in the water.

The cultural battlefield is swimming in it.

Metaphorically.

For now.

Not to be a "Mr. Grumpy Pants" about things, but I am compelled at this point to remind you (and me) that *we're* the ones most to blame for this smoldering slagheap of cultural wreckage known as America. The blood of this dying culture is first and foremost on American Christianity's hands. Judgment begins with the house of God.

As our most "conservative" "Christian" "leaders" continue to resist (and often rail against) the reality of God's Nature as revealed in His Word as *the binding reality for life in every realm of His creation*, we see enemies of Christ empowered, emboldened, and enabled to ravage the culture as never before. And man oh man, are they ever taking full advantage of this fish-in-a-barrel opportunity!

Millions of apathetic professing American Christians, convinced that all is lost anyway (so why bother?), seem quite content to avoid rocking the boat too much (if at all) while waiting for the rapture and watching the carnage unfold, offering up not even the tiniest token of resistance.

Thus, haters of God, holiness, and the holiness-pursuing people of God, grow in number, power attained, territory conquered, and crackpot crazy *confidence*.

They smell blood in the water. Lots of blood. And they want more.

As the American culture hemorrhages its last bits of life, the Christ-less culture of death and its Forces of Tolerance are increasingly willing to come out of the closet as something much more perverse than mere sexual deviants. So little do they fear credible Christian resistance at this point that they are now often outing themselves as overt, wide-open evangelists for *anti*-Christianity.

Just last month, *The Huffington Post* treated us to *I Have Come to Indoctrinate Your Children Into My LGBTQ Agenda (And I'm Not a Bit Sorry)*, which included the following tidbit of proud confession:

> *"I am here to tell you: All that time I said I wasn't indoctrinating anyone with my beliefs about gay and lesbian and bi and trans and queer people? That was a lie. All 25 years of my career as an LGBTQ activist, since the very first time as a 16-year-old I went and stood shaking and breathless in front of eleven people to talk about My Story, I have been on a consistent campaign of trying to change people's minds about us. I want to make them like us. That is absolutely my goal. I want to make your children like people like me and my family, even if that goes against the way you have interpreted the teachings of your religion."*

This is where the satanic approach to the pursuit of knowledge – the foundation of State-controlled children's education in America – was *always* going to take us. It was always intended as a platform for rebellion against God.

This overtly anti-Christian approach to the pursuit of truth has been enabled, encouraged, and even *defended* for so long from pulpits in America that things like public schools are now assumed to be perfectly viable options for the formation of little Christian children's minds and worldviews. So it is that American priests and pastors have played a great role in escorting our presently unfolding Orwellian nightmare onto the stage.

This path began long ago in American (and pre-United States) history. Once the Nature of God as revealed in His Word was set aside in favor of the shifting standards of man where the pursuit of law, government, and education are concerned, this is the destination that we chose. Of course, we are not yet seeing the final destination of this course, but we are beginning to get a good sniff of it.

In a recent post from Douglas Wilson, we get another warning and whiff of where this is all going:

"As I have already written, this issue is entirely and completely over a demand for approval. The homo-jihad is not demanding that we agree to function in the same economy together with them. We are more than willing to do that. Rather, they are demanding — not suggesting — that identification of their perversion with sin be made against the law. This includes everyone, everywhere, and it includes pulpits. So when they say "that would never happen," it should be pointed out that Christians are starting to get smart. We don't believe anything you say anymore.

So they are demanding that on such occasions where our participation in this same economy becomes tantamount to approval of the sin, and consequently a violation of our conscience, that we be required to violate our conscience. Their lusts trump our conscience."

So the sharks are in the water. They are growing in power and confidence.

Our culture is bleeding out. America is dying.

So what are *we* gonna do about it, Christian?

Shall we leave our children in State-controlled systems of "education" whose foundations are lifted straight from the serpent's tongue (see: Genesis 3)? Shall we refuse to *lovingly* confront and condemn such a system and submission to such a system as being inherently and obviously *sinful*?

Shall we continue to pretend that *we* have not sinned great sins in America by embracing and championing the freedom to worship false gods as a good thing while dismissing the Nature of God as revealed in His Word as our authority and standard in law, government, education, and everything else?

Who do we think that we are?

Who do we think that *He* is?

If our answers to those two questions are *biblical* (AKA "true"), and we *act accordingly* in faith by the grace of God, then – and *only* then – we will have the basis from which to find real hope and true restoration – even in this dark and dying culture.

If we truly repent, believe, and take up the Gospel-fueled Great Commission of Christ the King, we will stop bleeding, we will begin healing, and we will drive the enemies of the King from the cultural battlefields over which they now pridefully gloat.

4

SECTION FOUR

Our Preferred
Political Witchcraft

God bless America. And Planned Parenthood.

(Originally published at *Fire Breathing Christian* on July 21, 2015.)

Revelation leading to repentance can be a *very* hard thing. That's its nature.

But that doesn't make it any less a blessing from God.

Thankfully, these days we're getting a whole lotta revelation. Not much in the way of repentance yet, but God is graciously keeping the revelations coming anyway.

The latest wave of America-exposing truth has come by way of Planned Parenthood's shouldn't-be-at-all-surprising involvement in carefully protecting the ***parts*** of beautiful healthy little baby boys and girls while helping mothers murder these kids and then selling the preserved parts for profit.

Today there have been some timely reports reminding us of President Barack Obama's recent speech addressing Planned Parenthood, which he closed out by saying, "Thank you, Planned Parenthood. God bless you."

This all comes on the heels of America's proud plunge deeper into overt Statism by way of its Supreme Court's decision to uphold ObamaCare and then, in case there was any doubt left lingering as to our open hatred of God's Nature as revealed in His Word, the same court suicidally decreed the redefinition of the unalterable, God-ordained institution of marriage.

These things are then predictably used by the Pagan Right to paint Obama or Democrats or Leftists or whatever as the real problem. The real threat. The real enemy. The only cure for which is, of course, the Republican Party and Pagan "conservatism".

But what of this Pagan "conservatism"?

What of our encouraged America idolatry?

Has it not been used most effectively to convince "Christian conservatives" to embrace and proudly advocate counterfeit truths and concepts that are every bit as blasphemous as Obama's "God bless you, Planned Parenthood" line?

Have we not been convinced and do we not *proudly* proclaim that we have the "God-given right" to openly worship false gods?

Have we not been convinced and do we not *proudly* proclaim that we have the "God-given right" to freely speak blasphemy?

Have we not been convinced and do we not *proudly* proclaim that we have the "God-given right" to "legally" operate bu$ine$$e$ built for the purpose of "helping" women to sacrifice their own children on the altar of *convenience*?

All while feeling completely comfortable singing "God bless America", of course.

[insert "*U! S! A!*" chant here]

Is this not the American way?

Of course it is.

Then **is Barack Obama not the just judgment of God upon a people who will *not* have Him to rule over them?**

Remember: "God-given rights" are only as good – or as real – as the God giving them.

Which makes it fairly plain that the (temporarily) ruling (false) god in America is clearly *the American State*.

The Pagan Political Left and Pagan Political Right are two wings of the same dragon; two heads of the same beast that is the Corporate-owned and operated United States of America.

The sooner we realize that, the better.

Until we ditch the American pride, repent and submit to Christ as King *in practice*, we're gonna see and feel and smell more and more of the same...more and more revelations of just how profoundly pathetic, evil, and worthy of destruction we've become.

May God bless America with broken humility and total submission to Christ the King of creation...while there is yet time...

Jeb Bush makes the Pagan Right pitch on religion (again).

(Originally published at *Fire Breathing Christian* on May 11, 2014.)

Ever wonder what it looks like when one's politics defines one's Christianity, rather than the other way around?

Ever wonder what it looks like when *openly unbelieving* voices like Rush Limbaugh, Mark Levin, and the hordes of Neo-Cons at Fox News become the sages, icons and prophets to which vast swaths of professing Christians look to *first*, *most*, and *last* for culture-shaping political direction?

If you are wondering, you really shouldn't be; at least not in America. For tens of millions of politically active "conservative Christian" Americans, the notion of defining religion (including Christianity) by the light of secular (anti-Christian) approaches to politics, patriotism, economics and education is the norm. It's a given. It's just how things are done in "the real world".

For these folks, Jesus is Lord somewhere "out there" in the future or off in Heaven or in their little hearts or at prayer meetings or in the church choir, but He most certainly is *not* King *in practice* right here and now over *all* things – including politics, patriotism and most other concepts that are cherished by many of those who self-identify as "conservative Christians".

The "conservative Christian" distinction alone is anything but problematic in and of itself. It's a perfectly legitimate term conveying a perfectly legitimate worldview summary when used in a proper context. But the worldview that it is increasingly intended to convey (and justify) when used by millions upon millions of politically active professing Christians in America is a worldview in which Christianity – and Christ – play a *submissive* role to "conservatism" and the American State as they have been defined by the Pagan Right.

103

Thus, Christ as King *in practice* in the political, economic, business or patriotic realm right here and now is not a thing that these "conservative Christians" are into. Not at all and quite the contrary, actually. They tend to be inherently hostile to Christ's lordship in practice over any realm that they've set aside and reserved for rule by their favorite unbelieving secular leaders.

The Pagan Right has thoroughly co-opted the hearts and minds of legions of professing Christians in America, so much so that now the "freedom of religion" (as in, the "freedom" to worship any false god you like) is now understood by the masses to be a "God-given" right and a virtue upon which American identity (and pride) are built and proclaimed throughout creation. The fact that God – the real One – openly despises and has explicitly forbidden the religious pluralism at the heart of the religion of Americanism doesn't seem to phase these "conservative Christians" in the least. In fact, the more one shines light on this reality, the more these folks who define their religion in light of their politics seem to double down in favor of the very thing that God hates and has forbidden...all while claiming a love for Jesus and "Christian values" along the way, of course.

This is how wacky and warped things have become. Barring God-given brokenness and repentance on the part of these "conservative first" Christians, it's only going to get worse.

This is the context in which we roll into the next contrived/controlled presidential election cycle.

This time 'round, the Republican Establishment is offering up, among other things, another Bush.

Jeb Bush.

We'll get into more Jeb specifics in future posts, Lord willing. For now, it seems like a good idea to note and contemplate Jeb Bush's predictable regurgitation of the tried and true Pagan Right pitch on things like religion, freedom, liberty and Truth.

To that end, we turn to a piece run last week by McClatchy titled, *Bush courts evangelicals, defends religion in public life*:

Looking to win over skeptical evangelical voters, Jeb Bush pushed back Saturday against what he said are modern intrusions on religion as he lauded graduates and their families at Liberty University, a Christian college popular on the path to the Republican presidential nomination.

"Fashionable ideas and opinions – which these days can be a religion all by itself – have got a problem with Christians and their right of conscience," Bush told an audience of 34,000 in the school's football stadium.

First off, it's important to notice the purposefully vague appeal to "religion". The Pagan Right has done a masterful job of convincing its followers – many of whom claim Christianity – that "religion" is a synonym for "Christianity". It's never quite stated as clearly as that, of course (that's the point of being purposefully vague), but, at the end of the day, the Pagan Right is advocating for Islam and Allah the same treatment that it is advocating for Christianity and Christ. The appeal to "religion" is always made based on the American assumption of religious pluralism as a virtue, and in direct contradiction of the Word of the living, ruling God, which makes plain that He despises and will punish religious pluralism.

Just something to keep in mind there when you hear Pagan Right types go on about "defending religion"…

The phrase "right of conscience" is also interesting for a variety of reasons, perhaps most notably the fact that it appeals not to anything resembling the objective fact or truth of Christ as God and the reigning King of His creation. Instead, it appeals to that favorite "right" of the religious pluralist, that being the "right" to believe in and worship any way – and any god – that you like.

So we see where all of this "defense of religion" is going. (Hint: The same place that the Pagan Right has always had it going – *in defense of religious pluralism and in opposition to God.*)

Just in case you had any doubt, the following line makes plain once again the Pagan Right religious switcheroo:

"That makes it our problem, and the proper response is a forthright defense of the first freedom in our Constitution."

For Jeb & Company, the State is god in practice. For Jeb & Friends, religious pluralism is a virtue. And for the "conservative Christians" under sway of Pagan Right thought, nothing could be more "reasonable" or "right" here in the land of the free and the home of the NSA.

George Bush, George W. Bush, John McCain, Mitt Romney, Mike Huckabee...the list of Pagan Right "leaders" past and present goes on and on and on with proponents of American Statism and religious pluralism – both of which God despises.

One of the manners in which God has consistently punished a disobedient people is by way of wicked leadership. With every embrace and advocacy of a Pagan Right "leader" by professing Christians in America, those professing Christians lead the way in earning the wrath of God that is even now pouring down upon us.

Do you really believe that the Pagan Right will ever make a meaningful, *biblical*, uncompromising stand in defense of the Family?

Do you really think that the Pagan Right will ever make a meaningful, *biblical* reduction in the power of the State?

Do you really believe that the Pagan Right will ever remove children's "education" from the controlling hand of the State?

Do you really think that the Pagan Right will ever make a meaningful, *biblical* defense of the sanctity of sexuality?

Do you really believe that the Pagan Right will ever make a meaningful move toward biblical economics in place of the abomination that is in place now?

Of course not.

And why?

Because **the Pagan Right will never repent and submit to Christ as King in practice.**

Ever.

(Hint: This is why they are the "Pagan" Right; they may claim Christianity when convenient, but their worldview in application is obviously and thoroughly Pagan in nature.)

Until the Pagan Right is broken into repentance and submission to Christ as King in practice, they can and will only lead all who follow them deeper and deeper into darkness, despair, and death.

Christ as King is not merely the answer for some "out there" place in the future or "in our hearts" or in the privacy of our homes and church buildings. He is the one true hope and the inescapable, binding reality of *every* realm in His creation. And yes, that includes 2015 (and 2016) America.

Live, act and vote accordingly. You will give an account.

We the people...are not God.

(Originally published at *Fire Breathing Christian* on May 6, 2015.)

We the people are not God.

We the people are commanded to submit to Christ as King in practice.

We the people are not special or "exceptional" in any way that gives us a free pass to ignore, dismiss or reject Christ as King in practice.

We the people are commanded to repent of our past and present rebellion against Christ the King.

We the people are commanded to allow no false god to be openly worshiped in our land.

We the people are commanded to educate our children with Jesus Christ as the explicit core, source and object of the pursuit of knowledge.

We the people are commanded to discern and apply the distinct God-defined responsibilities and limitations of the God-ordained institutions of Family, Church and State.

We the people are commanded to learn and obey all that Christ the King has revealed of His Nature in His Word.

We the people are commanded to take every political, economic, educational, artistic, technological, cultural and civilizational thought captive to Christ.

We the people are commanded to make disciples of all nations, teaching everyone to love and obey Christ as King in practice.

We the people can do none of these things apart from the grace of God. We the people have been commanded *and equipped* by God to accomplish all of these otherwise impossible things through His Gospel-fueled Great Commission, secured and empowered by the blood of Christ the King, who will see His people through to victory:

> *And Jesus came and said to them, "**All authority in heaven and on earth has been given to me.** Go therefore and **make disciples of all nations**, baptizing them in the name of the Father and of the Son and of the Holy Spirit, **teaching them to observe all that I***

have commanded you*. And behold, I am with you always, to the end of the age."*

~ Matthew 28:18-20 (emphasis added)

5

SECTION FIVE

How An Americanized "Gospel" Got Us Here

A LIMP WRISTED GOSPEL

MAKES A LIMP WRISTED CULTURE

Limp Wristed Gospels Make Limp Wristed Cultures

(Originally published at *Fire Breathing Christian* on June 27, 2015.)

How's that "real world", "pragmatic political" approach to life working out for you, American Christian?

How's it *actually* shaping and molding the future of your children and grandchildren here in the "land of the free" and the home of the NSA?

How are all o' those *mountains* of votes and **billions** of dollars spent on "good conservative" Republicans panning out for ya?

How do things like "liberty", "freedom", "justice", "law", "family" and "marriage" feel to you now as they're increasingly separated from explicit subjugation to Christ the King for the sake of...*political pragmatism*?

Seriously.

How's it goin'?!

How's this "we the people" can do whatever we want thing treating ya?

Here's one interesting answer to that important question:

> *"No, the sky is not falling – not yet anyway – but with the Supreme Court ruling constitutionalizing same-sex marriage, the ground under our feet has shifted tectonically.*
>
> *It is hard to overstate the significance of the Obergefell decision – and the seriousness of the challenges it presents to orthodox Christians and other social conservatives.* ***Voting Republican and other failed culture war strategies are not going to save us now."***

These words were penned by Rod Dreher of *The American Conservative* and published online by *Time* yesterday.

And hard though they are, they actually understate the problem, and significantly so.

113

Christians in America have been lured in and swallowed up for generations now by an explicitly anti-Christian political puppet show production owned and operated by the very corporations and elites now showering their buildings and corporate logos with rainbow imagery in gleeful celebration of America's formal, full-blown profanation of marriage.

The culture is going the way that these rainbow-abusers like because *we* have bought into *their* spin on the gospel.

We have surrendered the life- and culture-restoring Gospel-fueled Great Commission of Jesus Christ and taken up instead any number of weak, fluffy, emotion-driven, self-centered counterfeits. We've got our Magic Christianity and our Candy Christianity; our Gospel in a Bottle and our Christianity in a Box; all aimed at making us feel better about the surrender of everything here to them because we have our magic "get out of hell free" card and nothing we do here "really matters anyway".

Consequently, we don't take the Great Commission seriously.

At all.

As a result of our apathy, laziness, and lack of cultural engagement *on Christ's terms*, we are now in a putrid bed of our own making, watching the American Corporate State go full-blown homo-advocate while shifting its political and economic power steadily into full-on Christian persecution mode.

The bottom line biblical (and therefore *inescapable*) truth is this: **Limp-wristed "gospels" make limp-wristed cultures.**

We are in this predicament because our Magic Christianity and Gospel in a Bottle brought us here.

Here's another biblical bottom line (and therefore *certain*) truth: **Until and unless we ditch (and repent of having ever embraced) our favorite false gospels and their preferred enemy-enabling approaches to politics, law, liberty and life, we are (and deserve to be) doomed.**

Until we ditch those pathetic counterfeits and take up the true, comprehensive, life- and culture-shaking Gospel-fueled Great Commission of Jesus Christ, we will continue to be as limp-wristed and destructive as anyone else in this train-wreck of a culture.

114

So let's lose the self-centered, emotion- and tradition-driven junk and get to building something *real* right here and now, all by the grace and all for the glory of the Author and Sustainer of all *true* reality.

Let's strive to *take* every artistic, economic, legal and political thought captive to Christ, as He has lovingly commanded and equipped His people to do, so that we might have the families, homes, communities and cultures that Pagan Political Right and Pagan Political Left "leaders" and "experts" always claim to want but never can and never will deliver.

Let's drop the liberty-, freedom-, privacy- and life-crushing gospel of American Corporate Statism and take up the supernatural life- and culture-resurrecting Gospel of Christ the King:

> *And Jesus came and said to them, **"All authority in heaven and on earth has been given to me. Go therefore and make disciples of all nations, baptizing them in the name of the Father and of the Son and of the Holy Spirit, teaching them to observe all that I have commanded you. And behold, I am with you always, to the end of the age."***
>
> *~ Matthew 28:18-20*

Little Gospel Syndrome and the Death of American Culture

(Originally published at *Fire Breathing Christian* on September 10, 2015.)

Wouldn't it be great if people took God seriously?

Wouldn't it be great if people took God seriously enough to take His Word seriously?

In *detail*, I mean.

As in, *all of it*.

As in, out of a true love for Him (see: John 14:15).

Wouldn't it be great if the professing Christian church in America led the culture in this direction...instead of away from it?

The increasingly disintegrating American culture is not primarily a product of liberalism, however much secular "conservatives" may say otherwise. It's not primarily the product of ignorance, however much the "education"-minded may imagine otherwise. And it's not primarily the result of hedonism or materialism, however much the "hyper-spiritual" among us may proclaim to the contrary. The dying American culture is first and foremost a product of the professing Christian church's abandonment of the full, life- and world-defining Gospel of Jesus Christ. In making the Gospel just about our personal salvation and letting the rest of creation go to hell without too much concern or opposing effort on our part, we have abandoned the Great Commission and denied the nature of the true, supernatural Gospel of Christ.

In considering ourselves "good to go" with a mere profession of faith accompanied by "good works" like regular church attendance, Bible readings, and other Christian-ish activities, we've traded in the comprehensive Christian life and worldview for a self-centered, comfortable, easy path of disengagement and pre-emptive surrender. We've traded in the life- and culture-transforming mission of the Gospel-fueled Great Commission for a life of minimal effort and minimal (if any) commitment to "take *every* thought captive" (see: 2 Corinthians

10:5) and become disciples who actively strive to **obey all that Christ has commanded** (see: Matthew 28:18-20).

Where the Gospel of Jesus touches literally everything, we have decided to keep our version of it neatly sequestered and safely "in its place", relegating it to largely ornamental status. We like to admire and read Scripture about how awesome it is, and talk about how awesome it is, but when it comes to application…well…did I mention that it is a beautiful ornament?

It's an ornament that we like to keep in a display case and show off "at the right times", with "the right people" and in "the right places", but when it comes to bringing its purposeful, everything-defining light into contact with everything, as Christ has clearly commanded His people to do and as the very nature of the true Gospel requires, well…we like to keep it simple…and vague…

We love to say, "Jesus died for sinners!"

But we hate to define sin.

We love to say, "Repent and be saved!"

But if we won't define sin, what is it that people are supposed to repent of, exactly?

If **failing to do what God has commanded** and **doing what God has forbidden** is sin, then we obviously can't have a coherent, vibrant, effective Gospel presentation if we are not about the business of identifying what those sins are in detail in light of His Word, can we?

Even the twelve-steppers understand that the first *necessary* step to solving a problem is *acknowledging that it exists*, right?

If someone asks, "Is homosexual intimacy a sin?", most of us have little trouble saying that such activity is indeed sinful.

Yet if someone asks something along the lines of, "Is it okay for me to send my five year old off to the State for what we all know is an explicitly anti-Christian 'education'?", we often hem and haw. Or, even worse (and far more commonly), we say something like, "Sure. Go ahead. Just be sure to use the comparatively little time you have with them to try and at least *begin* to compensate for some of the satanic spin on the pursuit of knowledge that they are being modeled and molded to emulate and embrace all day long each weekday."

118

And then we wonder why each successive generation of professing American Christians is less Christian, more liberal, and more Statist than the last.

Has God spoken any less clearly on the necessity of Christ as the explicit core of children's education than He has on the subject of homosexuality?

Could our abandonment of His Word in the one area be the primary reason we are experiencing so much hellishness in the other?

Has God not spoken clearly as to the nature, purpose, and application of law, economics, and civil government?

Has God not spoken clearly and sufficiently to us so that we might understand and profitably pursue *every* good work possible in His creation?

> *All Scripture is breathed out by God and profitable for **teaching**, for **reproof**, for **correction**, and for **training in righteousness**, that the man of God may be **complete, equipped for <u>every</u> good work**.*
>
> ~ 2 Timothy 3:16-17 (emphasis added)

The Gospel is *not* all about us.

It's all about *Him*.

It's all about Him restoring *everything*.

It's all about Him restoring everything by His grace through His Spirit-filled people in accordance with His Gospel-fueled Great Commission.

The sooner we ditch and repent of having ever embraced the pathetic little self-centered "Gospel in a Bottle" that we've allowed to lead our culture to where it is now, the better.

Big Government, Big Materialism, Big Liberalism, and Big Hedonism are not what's killing America. Not primarily, anyway.

Little Gospel Syndrome is what's killing America.

6

SECTION SIX

For the Love of **True** Liberty

GETTING OUR FLAGS IN ORDER

How to truly love (and really save) America.

(Originally published at *Fire Breathing Christian* on December 17, 2014.)

What does love mean?

What does it mean to love someone or something?

Most of us would describe love first as an intense emotion or feeling of endearment toward someone or something. Most of us would describe loving a person or thing then in very subjective, emotion-driven terms.

And most of us would therefore be very, very wrong.

Love – as all other concepts at the heart of human understanding and life – is only rightly defined by Scripture.

When we begin to define or understand a term as important as love anywhere but Scripture, we are beginning in darkness. And when we begin in that darkness using our feelings as a primary guide, well...it only gets worse from there.

So it is that ever-increasing darkness has become the norm in America.

Through generations of purposeful separation from Truth by way of everything from State-controlled "education" to Corporate-controlled pop-culture, we have been systematically encouraged to embrace and nurture a subjective, self-referential, emotion- and feeling-driven understanding of love (and everything else).

For more liberal, leftist, or openly pagan types, this self-defined, self-serving "love" touches, defines, and fundamentally corrupts the things most dear to their unbelieving hearts. So it is that everything from rank sexual perversion to open appeals to Statism are all advocated in the name of "love".

For conservative types, including a great many professing Christians who regularly attend the most conservative of "Bible believing" churches, their self-defined, self-serving "love" tends to inspire idolatry of things like America and patriotism itself. One interesting (and revealing) bit of overlap between these folks and their leftists brothers and sisters is that they too, in the name of their "love" of country, end up as open advocates of Statism. They definitely prefer that it be a Republican-led Statism, but it is Statism nonetheless.

In this, both conservative and liberal unbelievers (many of whom claim Christianity) become passionate advocates of things like "freedom" and "liberty", all defined and understood through the anti-Christian foundation upon which they are built. So the Left and the Right end up championing many of the same terms, all of which are equally (though differently) distinct from their biblical presentation.

The reason for this rather profound overlap between the Left and Right secular views is that they have been born of the same rebellion. They have been built upon the same fundamental rejection of Christ as Lord *in practice* right here and right now in every realm of His creation...including language, politics, economics, and education.

Once an understanding or definition of love, patriotism, America, or anything else is severed from an explicit connection to Christ as its essential-life-preserving core, then that thing becomes dead and death to all that it touches.

So what does this tell us about true love?

How do we truly love a person, or a group of people like America?

How do we practice God-honoring (and therefore life-preserving) patriotism, politics, economics, and education?

Well, the good news is that there is a simple, clear answer: We begin by actively subjecting our understanding of all things to the nature of Christ as revealed in His Word.

We must begin with Christ.

Purposefully.

Clearly.

Publicly.

Always.

We really and truly *must* begin and remain centered on Christ *personally* if we are to ever find true, lasting beauty, peace, and prosperity in any realm of His creation.

However much we may be ignorant, unsure, or confused when it comes to details, we must openly, publicly, and persistently begin every significant pursuit of understanding by making a direct appeal to Christ as personally revealed in His perfect Word.

That is the essential first step to understanding, and then pursuing, true love for a person or a people.

And that is the one step that *every* secular so-called "conservative", liberal and libertarian source, expert, and prognosticator will *always* dutifully strive to avoid (and steer us away from) at all costs.

They will not submit to the lordship of Christ.

This really couldn't be more clear or obvious – just tune in to CNN, Fox News, MSNBC, Rush Limbaugh, Sean Hannity, Mark Levin or any number of other cogs in the controlled, contrived "conservative"/liberal media machine. They are all ultimately and always aimed at what all satanic/secular thought advocates: Distraction from Christ as the essential personal core of life (or any part of it).

And to this we must say, "no."

And, "repent".

We must lovingly confront this widespread, culture-killing rebellion with the Gospel of Jesus Christ the King.

That is love.

That is the truly loving thing to do.

And it will require from each of us first, by God's grace, a personal desire to repent of *our* propagation of the satanic worldview that is now strangling the culture before our eyes.

We have enabled and adored this beast.

We have played its game…and loved playing it.

We have failed to hold the realms of language, politics, economics, and education close to Christ as their essential life-giver, and in our failure *we* have promoted the death of each of those things.

We have led America to darkness.

We have ruined patriotism through our idolatry of America.

We have much to repent of before we can lead this land and its people to resurrection through the Gospel-fueled Great Commission, but the great news is that this is exactly why our Lord has placed us in this place and at this time.

We are here for great purpose. We have before us now the opportunity to repent of *our* idolatry and destroy *our* idols as a leading example, so that we might through our grace-fueled obedience inspire others to do the same and actually, truly save this culture…one supernatural salvation at a time.

With this incredible (and most challenging) situation in mind, please consider the following passages:

> *Then Jesus told his disciples, "If anyone would come after me, let him deny himself and take up his cross and follow me. For whoever would save his life will lose it, but whoever loses his life for my sake will find it. For what will it profit a man if he gains the whole world and forfeits his soul? Or what shall a man give in return for his soul?*

> *~ Matthew 16:24-26*

> **"Do not think that I have come to bring peace to the earth. I have not come to bring peace, but a sword.** *For I have come to set a man against his father, and a daughter against her mother, and a daughter-in-law against her mother-in-law. And a person's enemies will be those of his own household.* **Whoever loves father or mother more than me is not worthy of me, and whoever loves son or daughter more than me is not worthy of me. And whoever does not take his cross and follow me is not worthy of me. Whoever finds his life will lose it, and whoever loses his life for my sake will find it.***"*

> *~ Matthew 10:34-39 (bold emphasis added)*

We are here and now in this desperate hour to proclaim and apply the truth that salvation is only possible through the person of Christ the King.

That salvation covers everything in His creation, right on down to the language.

We are here to save "love" from perversion.

We are here to save "patriotism" from corruption.

126

We are here to save America from death.

And we are here to save those things by bringing them to Him; by subjecting them to His loving authority and life-giving perfection. We are here to demonstrate and advocate that everything, including our patriotism, is to be subject to the lordship of Christ the King.

We are here to learn together, by God's grace, what that means in detail as we study and submit to Him along the ongoing path of sanctification, but we are all obligated to openly, publicly, and relentlessly begin every serious pursuit of every serious subject by striving to publicly, purposefully define it in light of the Person of Christ as revealed in His perfect Word.

So when we are told that anti-Christian approaches to education, politics, economics, or love are "just the way the world works" or "what we have to put up with here", we must lovingly and clearly *confront* that contention and *correct it* in light of the Word of God.

This is our Great Commission:

> And Jesus came and said to them, "**All authority in heaven and on earth has been given to me**. Go therefore and **make disciples of all nations**, baptizing them in the name of the Father and of the Son and of the Holy Spirit, **teaching them to observe all that I have commanded you**. And behold, I am with you always, to the end of the age."
>
> ~ Matthew 28:18-20 (bold emphasis added)

This is how we *rightly* love.

This is how we can *actually* and *truly* save America, by God's grace, for His glory, and to our eternal benefit.

And *there is no other way*...

...and we of all people, as Christians, shouldn't want it any other way.

There is a culture raging, burning, and dying all around us, filled with people in desperate need of loving confrontation and correction through the Gospel-fueled Great Commission.

May God grace His people with the desire and opportunity to lead the way to Him through personal repentance and obedience in every realm of life right here and right now…while there is yet time.

Roaring into Post-America Christianity

(Originally published at *Fire Breathing Christian* on April 11, 2015.)

Christ is the perfection and embodiment of justified *optimism*.

Satan is the epitome and lowly priest of delusional *pessimism*.

The present, all-encompassing rule of Christ as King over every realm of His creation is the most invigorating, inspiring, optimism-igniting truth that can wash over the mind, spirit, and soul of man. This is why everything that the enemy does and hopes for centers on replacing the reality of Christ as King with *doubt* in Christ as *that* King.

The enemy plants, nurtures, and feeds on this doubt. Doubt is the means by which he strives to sustain (and at times grow) his fleeting, phony little kingdom. He cannot exist where the light of Christ is embraced and applied, and he knows it. Thus, everything for him begins with and is utterly reliant upon the cultivation of doubt – and not his doubt, but *ours*.

To that end, he strives mightily to have us focus on *anything but Christ* as our source of hope and life-defining optimism, so that it might be replaced with life-dimming pessimism. If we can be nudged to build and look to idols rather than Christ, the enemy has all that he needs to direct us in an anti-Christian, counter-Kingdom direction. He has all that he needs to introduce and build *doubt* in Christ as King.

The doubt sown by the enemy brings a spirit of pessimism, apathy, laziness, and surrender to those in whom it takes root. That seed of doubt then sprouts, inspiring ever-increasing suspicion, rejection and perversion of Christ's authority in whichever order or combination necessary to cement pessimism in place while securing a path to more of the same in the future.

This process of building doubt, suspicion, rejection and perversion of Christ's Nature has been rolling along almost unchallenged on a massive scale in our land for hundreds of years now. For those of us living in America today, it's hard to imagine life any other way or charting a future for our culture that follows anything other than a downward path. Yet is wasn't always and will not always be this way. Once upon a time, even in America, there was great optimism about the prospects for increasingly Christ-honoring culture and civilization.

From where did such optimism come? What was its basis? Why did people think – *and live* – in such a powerfully *optimistic* manner?

They did so *because they had great faith in Christ **as** King right here and now*. Not just as King out there in the future somewhere. Not just as King in their hearts. Not just as King at the church house or in the prayer closet. They believed in Christ as King over everything here, now, and forevermore. Thus, they weren't apathetic or lazy about advancing the Kingdom right here and now and they weren't riding things out huddled up together in little Christian ghettos waiting to be raptured away. They were actively engaging life and culture in every area by the grace of God, for the glory of God, and for the advancement of His Kingdom.

Right now in America, you and I are still (barely) coasting along on the last bits of remaining cultural residue left by their faith in action.

They actually believed what their King said and they actually lived in accordance with His Great Commission:

> *And Jesus came and said to them,* **"All authority in heaven and on earth has been given to me. Go therefore and make disciples of all nations, baptizing them in the name of the Father and of the Son and of the Holy Spirit, teaching them to observe all that I have commanded you. And behold, I am with you always, to the end of the age."**
>
> *~ Matthew 28:18-20*

Obviously, in this context, we have fallen far. Where once our forebears – Pilgrims and Puritans past – had, by God's grace, a serious taste, appetite, and zeal for the matchlessly invigorating, inspiring, optimism-igniting truth that Christ *is* King and that His Gospel-fueled Great Commission really, truly does radically and supernaturally transform people and all that they touch, we are now a people and a culture almost entirely defined by a satanic pride/pessimism paradigm.

We look to America, American traditions, favorite secular experts, our communities, families, friends and ultimately ourselves as the basis for measuring everything, including prospects for the future, rather than looking to and actively obeying Christ *as* King. When we take that satanic approach – when we look to our idols instead of the one true King – we water and nurture the doubt that then makes us into the apathetic, lazy, culturally-disengaged, preemptively-surrendering "Christians" that have come to define the modern American professing Christian sub-culture and lead the broader American culture straight to hell.

Addressing the life and culture-dooming sloth and denial of Christ on the part of professing Christians and calling them, by the grace of God, to awake, repent, and *believe*, is a theme of what we are trying to do here at *Fire Breathing Christian.*

Just this week we've chronicled things like the increasingly militant homo-jihad against the Christian worldview, America's ongoing systematic mass murder of children for convenience and profit, and witches leading legislators in prayer at the Iowa state capitol. We've also reminded ourselves that rejecting His Nature as revealed in His Word as the basis for law in the land is suicidally stupid and that the devil can only hold that which Christians leave in his hands. We've considered all of these things with the aim of becoming more comfortable with and enthusiastic about Christ as King – whether there happens to be a United States of America for much longer or not. Post-Christian America is here, and while that may be sad and tragic in many ways, post-America Christianity is assured, and that beautiful truth should inspire us as nothing else can.

For those who would like to see America saved or somehow restored, that can and will never happen by looking within for salvation. America will not be saved by American principles, American virtues, conservative politics, the Republican Party, or anything else that is not explicitly connected to and explicitly submissive to Jesus Christ as Lord *in practice.*

That is the unbreakable reality of the situation.

There is one – and only one – path to true restoration, and that path is the Nature of Christ as revealed in His perfect, sufficient Word.

This is the dividing line between life and death – for America and anything or anyone else in God's creation.

This great and certain divide that separates light and life from darkness and death is the thing that the enemy strives to obscure through those seeds of pessimism-enabling doubt.

Jesus Christ, the reigning King of creation, to whom **all** authority has been given in heaven and **on earth**, *is the most **purposefully divisive** force in all of history*. His Gospel command to repent and believe is just that: *a command*. It is not a request. It is a loving demand for the complete and unconditional surrender of those who deserve no such opportunity. It is a demand to reject one's self as god and submit to the lordship of Christ in every detail and every realm of life.

> *"Do not think that I have come to bring peace to the earth. I have not come to bring peace, but a sword. For I have come to set a man against his father, and a daughter against her mother, and a daughter-in-law against her mother-in-law. And a person's enemies will be those of his own household. Whoever loves father or mother more than me is not worthy of me, and whoever loves son or daughter more than me is not worthy of me. And whoever does not take his cross and follow me is not worthy of me. Whoever finds his life will lose it, and whoever loses his life for my sake will find it."*
>
> *~ Jesus, in Matthew 10:34-39*

One day soon, His wrath will come upon those who – like America – even now cling to their pride and imagined lordship over their own lives. In the meantime, His Gospel command goes forth by way of His obedient people, propelling their growth in number and inspiring them to bring every aspect of creation that they touch more and more into conformity with the King's Nature as revealed in His Word, all by His grace, all for His glory, and all to the eternal benefit of His faithful, chosen people.

We don't need America.

Never have. Never will.

America needs Christians – Christians who will do everything that they are able with everything that they have been given in order to advance the Gospel-fueled Great Commission in every realm of life, culture, and civilization.

Christ the King doesn't need America.

America needs Christ – Christ as King *in practice*.

Victory is ours! Christ *is* King! Let America repent or suffer the consequences. Either way, His rule and Kingdom go on forevermore, all for the glory of God and all to the eternal benefit of His people.

This is the banner reality under which we must clearly march, fight, and advance His Kingdom.

This is the flag under which we must faithfully proclaim the Gospel command to repent and believe.

This is the truth that prevents us from pessimistically shambling, slinking, or skulking fearfully, with our heads hung low, into the likely post-America Christian world to come. This is the truth that instead enables us to ravage and route the enemy on every battlefield in every realm of culture and civilization, all by the grace and for the glory of the King.

Like the old hymn says, "Judah's Lion has burst his chains!"

This is truth that makes us roar…and our enemies tremble.

7

SECTION SEVEN

The Gospel's Victory
Over Satanic "Liberty"

What does Jesus bring to politics, education, law, and economics?

(Originally published at *Fire Breathing Christian* on October 20, 2014.)

The Bible is loaded with foundational statements that are bizarre, offensive and often quite disgusting to the unbelieving ear.

We are commanded to "eat Christ's flesh and drink His blood". We are told that He is "the bread of life", "the Word made flesh", and that He is "the way, the truth, and the life" personified.

Echoes of these phrases bounce around the American country side regularly, particularly on Sundays, yet they are rarely, if ever, seriously contemplated, applied, or "fleshed out", so to speak. This dismissive approach to these fundamental truths of biblical Christianity has been embraced by most professing Christians for generations now. Lip service and autopilot amen-ing has replaced vigorous pursuit and application of the *personified* truth of Jesus Christ in even some of the most self-described "conservative" and "Bible preaching" churches.

We must "eat His flesh and drink His blood"? *What?!*

He is "the bread of life"? Ummm…*okay…*

He's "the way, the truth, and the life"? Yeah, we have an easier time with that one, but what does it actually *mean*? What are its implications? Do we even care?

The importance of these ideas and their relationship to our current cultural slide into oblivion makes itself plain 99% of the time that the typical American "Christian" is challenged to think biblically along these lines.

Just try to seriously relate a discussion of politics, economics, art, or children's education directly to the nature of Christ as revealed in His Word as the standard by which the realm of life under consideration is to be tested and see what happens.

You're roughly 10,000 times more likely to be met with a confused, frustrated, or even angry glare from the typical Christian in America than you are to hear anything like, "Of course, everything begins with Christ, so let's consider this in light of what He has revealed on the subject in His perfect word."

Actually measure politics by Christ?

Are you kidding?!

Art, law, business, economics…

Are you some kind of fanatic or something?!

Children's education…

Oh, just shut up and go away, already. You aren't even living in the real world.

While it is only to be expected that unbelievers would object (often mockingly and/or angrily) to Christ's nature as being the actual binding standard against which everything is to be measured and tested right here and now, the sad reality is that the vast majority of professing Christians have joined their unbelieving friends, co-workers, teachers, and family members in this mocking, dismissive rejection of the only standards capable of bringing and sustaining true life, peace, and stability to any realm in God's creation.

Keep the Bible talk vague, and these professing Christians are fine with it.

They have little trouble singing, nodding in agreement, or otherwise affirming that "Jesus is Lord". As for any detailed *application* of that claim, well…they're not very interested in that. Not very interested at all.

Not only are they disinterested in seeking and applying the lordship of Christ in life in any detail, but, whenever pressed, they are often just about as hostile to the idea as their openly unbelieving friends. This then begs the question: Are they true believers?

Are they actually Christians?

Not surprisingly, this perfectly good and proper question itself is often reviled by the same religious folks who bristle at the suggestion that Christ is at this very moment the binding, authoritative personal standard against which all art, law, philosophy, economics, and educational pursuits are to be measured and tested.

Yet Scripture again and again presents and then answers the "how do I know if I am really saved?" question by pointing to the test of true love for Christ as defined in His perfect Word: If we love Him, we will have a

138

deep desire to learn and apply everything that He has commanded – we will, as the Scripture repeatedly states – strive, by His grace, to learn and keep His commandments.

We are saved by the grace of God alone through faith alone in Christ alone. Our works contribute *nothing* to either our attaining or maintaining salvation. Salvation is all of God, **and** we are saved *unto* good works, the active pursuit of holiness in every realm of life, and the Great Commission to make like-minded (as in "Christ-minded") disciples of all the nations and teach them to do *all* that Christ the King has commanded (see: Matthew 28).

This, quite obviously, applies to everything that He has commanded with regard to economics, education, politics, sexuality, and everything else.

By God's grace through the Gospel, we are supernaturally transformed into what Scripture calls "new creatures in Christ". As a result of this supernatural transformation, we are given a new desire to pursue the God-centered holiness we once hated and resist the self-centered sin and rebellion to which we were previously enslaved.

In this transformation we abandon the pathetic pursuit of lordship over our own lives and we happily submit to Christ the King *as* King.

This is all coherently and repeatedly presented throughout the New Testament, yet the concept of actual, right-now subjugation to Christ as King in all things and in all realms of life is utterly repugnant to many professing Christians…which means that, according to Scripture, it is quite likely that these professing believers are not actual Christians at all.

Which is all the more reason to share the Gospel. While we cannot know with certainty who is and who is not saved on this side of eternity, we can and do know this: Every unbeliever desperately needs to hear and submit to the whole, undiluted Gospel of Jesus Christ the King, and every believer has need of hearing the same supernaturally beautiful and powerful truth again and again as a reminder.

Every serious consideration of *every* significant subject must begin with Christ as the clear, defining, and life-giving standard by which it is to be measured and understood.

Thus, *any* serious conversation on *any* significant issue of the day is a vital, much needed opportunity to proclaim and apply the Gospel and Great Commission.

So what does Jesus bring to politics, education, law, and economics?

Life.

He gives them true *life*. Insofar as they conform to His nature, they are good; they will live and inspire life in every good and meaningful sense. Insofar as they dismiss or abandon His nature, they lead to darkness and death.

We are lovingly told to "eat His flesh and drink His blood" because He is the very foundation of all true, abundant life in every material and immaterial aspect of His creation. He really *is* truth. He really *is* life. *Personally.*

This is why His nature as revealed in His Word is essential to a right understanding or pursuit of anything in His creation. Every material and immaterial thing is utterly dependent upon His nature in this way. Art, music, family, law, philosophy, sexuality and everything else can *only* be rightly understood and pursued in light of and subjugation to Him *personally* – as revealed in His Word.

That's how things work in *His* creation.

That's how it always has been and that's how it always will be.

Our missing (or choosing to miss) that rather ginormous point is exactly why we are where we are right now as a culture.

To claim that Christ can be "set aside" as anything but the essential core in any realm of life is to openly invite death and destruction into that realm…which is exactly what we've done in economics, education, family life, religion, politics, art…the list goes on and covers every aspect of our proud, dying culture.

To truly live in "the real world" is to submit to the life-sustaining, truth-defining nature of Christ the King. To pretend to be living in the real world while advocating any other approach to living is life-, family- and culture-destroying *foolishness*…no matter how much you participate in churchy activities and no matter what your professional pastor tells you.

140

The "real world" and everything in and around it is entirely owned and defined by Christ.

That's the reality that we are to faithfully proclaim and apply at every opportunity that He gives us in every area of life.

That is the only truth upon which anything (or anyone) in this dying culture can actually be saved.

The devil only holds what we leave in his hands.

(Originally published at *Fire Breathing Christian* on April 7, 2015.)

What does Satan own?

What does the devil control?

What does the enemy dominate?

Only what we leave in his wicked, pathetic little hands. Put another way: The devil only holds what we let him keep.

Our mission – our Great Commission – is to press the crown rights of King Jesus in every realm of His creation right here and now. By His grace-fueled Gospel we have been commanded and equipped to become and propagate disciples who will strive – *all by His grace* – to increasingly conform every area of their lives to His Nature as revealed in His Word, thus transforming everything that they touch into a more and more Christ-honoring area of life.

Judah's Lion Has Burst His Chains

I love the hymn that proclaims the beautiful, cosmos-shaking, enemy-terrifying truth that "Judah's lion has burst his chains"! Death could not contain Him and nothing can deny Him.

The serpent's head has been crushed and the enemy is bleeding out before our eyes. Victory has been secured and is unfolding as that defeated enemy fades away.

Judah's Lion has chosen His people by His grace through His Gospel and His Great Commission to make His victory ever clearer and clearer throughout His creation.

Art, math, law, economics, business, and education – they're all *His*, along with *everything else*. We are here to make that plain, in word and application.

That's our job…all by His grace, all for His glory, and all to our eternal benefit.

In-between yesterday's *From Post-Christian America to Post-America Christianity* post and what will, Lord willing, be a *Part 2* follow-up later this week, it seemed like a good time to pause, remind ourselves, and marinate in the important truth that greater is He who is in us than he who is in the world (see: 1 John 4:4).

So it is that when we submit ourselves to God, we can effectively resist the devil, driving him from the field of battle. When the devil encounters a biblically obedient Christian, it is the devil, *not* the Christian, who is compelled to flight, retreat, and loss of ground (see: James 4:7).

How contrary is this to what most American Christians have been pitched and programmed to hide under when it comes to the relationship between the devil, Christians, and ground to be gained from (or lost to) the enemy here and now?

Consider the following passages:

> *By this you know the Spirit of God: every spirit that confesses that Jesus Christ has come in the flesh is from God, and every spirit that does not confess Jesus is not from God. This is the spirit of the antichrist, which you heard was coming and now is in the world already. Little children, you are from God and have overcome them, for **he who is in you is greater than he who is in the world**. They are from the world; therefore they speak from the world, and the world listens to them. We are from God. Whoever knows God listens to us; whoever is not from God does not listen to us. By this we know the Spirit of truth and the spirit of error.*
>
> *~ 1 John 4:2-6 (emphasis added)*

> *Submit yourselves therefore to God. **Resist the devil, and he will flee from you.***
>
> *~ James 4:7 (emphasis added)*

These are but samples from one of the great themes in Scripture – a theme that has been almost completely abandoned and forgotten by the professing Christian sub-culture in America. We have drifted (or, more appropriately, *run*) from this truth so hard for so long in America that today far more professing American "conservative" Christians are prone to mock this matchlessly empowering truth than they are to embrace it.

The crushed, dying serpent must laugh at – and greatly appreciate – such accommodating foolishness, which allows him to pretend and hold onto territory for just a little while longer.

The real world changing, supernatural power of the Gospel-fueled Great Commission is something that we desperately need to recover, which is why the enemies of Christ are so desperate to see it remain in its largely abandoned and forgotten state.

But those enemies are getting nervous.

They're getting concerned.

Here and there in the culture – including the professing Christian sub-culture – enemies from within and outside of the church are becoming more and more desperate in their disparaging of the authority of Christ as King and those who would dare to proclaim and apply Christ's comprehensive lordship right here and now in what they imagine and claim to be "the devil's world".

But it isn't working.

His people, by His grace, are on the move.

The Gospel – the *whole* Gospel – in all of it's supernatural life- and culture-transforming glory, will *not* be contained.

It will *not* be denied.

Because *He* will not be denied.

Judah's lion has burst his chains.

Jesus Conquers Everything

(Originally published at *Fire Breathing Christian* on June 13, 2015.)

There's nothing like serving the living, active, reigning King of Creation on a lifelong mission of eternal consequence that He has *personally* called and *perfectly* equipped you to *assuredly* accomplish by His grace, for His glory, and to the eternal benefit of His people.

I mean, **WOW!**

Can I get an "amen!"?

[I know you're reading this and I'm not likely to hear, but that's not the point. Please just humor me.]

Along these lines earlier this year in *Roaring into Post-America Christianity* and *The devil only holds what we leave in his hands.* I wrote about what to me is one of the most supercool, supernaturally inspiring bits o' man-written lyrical genius *ever*:

> . . . *I love the hymn that proclaims the beautiful, cosmos-shaking, enemy-terrifying truth that* **"Judah's lion has burst his chains!"** *Death could not contain Him and nothing can deny Him.*
>
> *The serpent's head has been crushed and the enemy is bleeding out before our eyes. Victory has been secured and is unfolding as that defeated enemy fades away.*
>
> *Judah's Lion has chosen His people by His grace through His Gospel and His Great Commission to make His victory ever clearer and clearer throughout His creation.*
>
> *Art, math, law, economics, business, and education – they're all His, along with everything else. We are here to make that plain, in word and application.*
>
> *That's our job…all by His grace, all for His glory, and all to our eternal benefit.*

With these ideas percolating in my perpetually awestruck little head, I thought it'd be good to take a moment to bask in the glow of some of the many clear passages proclaiming (and therefore assuring us of) Christ the King's present reign and unfolding domination of His creation in time and history.

So check this out…and bask in the glow…:

The LORD says to my Lord: "<u>Sit at my right hand, until I make your enemies your footstool.</u>" The LORD sends forth from Zion your mighty scepter. Rule in the midst of your enemies! Your people will offer themselves freely on the day of your power, in holy garments; from the womb of the morning, the dew of your youth will be yours. The LORD has sworn and will not change his mind, "You are a priest forever after the order of Melchizedek." The Lord is at your right hand; he will shatter kings on the day of his wrath. He will execute judgment among the nations, filling them with corpses; he will shatter chiefs over the wide earth. He will drink from the brook by the way; therefore he will lift up his head.

~ Psalm 110 (emphasis added)

The Lord is to be seated at the right hand of the Father *until* His enemies are made His footstool. Jesus is this Lord who is seated in that place, awaiting His enemies to be made His footstool, as the Father has promised:

*Who is to condemn? Christ Jesus is the one who died—more than that, who was raised—**who is at the right hand of God**, who indeed is interceding for us.*

~ Romans 8:34 (emphasis added)

*He is the radiance of the glory of God and the exact imprint of his nature, and **he upholds the universe by the word of his power**. After making purification for sins, **he <u>sat down at the right hand of the Majesty</u> on high***

~ Hebrews 1:3 (emphasis added)

*Now the point in what we are saying is this: we have such a high priest, one who **<u>is seated at the right hand of the throne of the Majesty</u> in heaven***

~ Hebrews 8:1 (emphasis added)

*. . . that he worked in Christ when he raised him from the dead and **seated him at his right hand in the heavenly places**, far **<u>above all rule and authority and power and dominion</u>**, and above every name that is named, **not only <u>in this age</u>** but also in the one to come. And he put **<u>all</u> things under his feet** and gave him as head over all things to the church, which is his body, the fullness of him who fills all in all.*

~ Ephesians 1:20-23 (emphasis added)

*. . . Jesus Christ, who has gone into heaven and **is at the right hand of God**, with **angels, authorities, and powers <u>having been subjected to him</u>**.*

~ 1 Peter 3:21-22 (emphasis added)

*This Jesus God raised up, and of that we all are witnesses. **Being therefore exalted at the right hand of God**, and having received from the Father the promise of the Holy Spirit, he has poured out this that you yourselves are seeing and hearing. For David did not ascend into the heavens, but he himself says, **"'The Lord said to my Lord, "Sit at my right hand, until I make your enemies your footstool."'"***

~ Acts 2:32-35 (emphasis added)

Do we see the theme here? Whether we do or not, it continues…and gets even better:

> *Now while the Pharisees were gathered together, Jesus asked them a question, saying, "What do you think about the Christ? Whose son is he?" They said to him, "The son of David." He said to them, "How is it then that David, in the Spirit, calls him Lord, saying,* **"The Lord said to my Lord, "Sit at my right hand, until I put your enemies under your feet""?** *If then David calls him Lord, how is he his son?" And no one was able to answer him a word, nor from that day did anyone dare to ask him any more questions.*
>
> ~ *Matthew 22:41-46 (emphasis added)*

Now read the thematic passage quoted again and again in the Word and by the Word made flesh:

> *Why do the nations rage and the peoples plot in vain? The kings of the earth set themselves, and the rulers take counsel together, against the LORD and against his Anointed, saying, "Let us burst their bonds apart and cast away their cords from us." He who sits in the heavens laughs; the Lord holds them in derision. Then he will speak to them in his wrath, and terrify them in his fury, saying, "As for me, I have set my King on Zion, my holy hill." I will tell of the decree:* **The LORD said to me, "You are my Son; today I have begotten you.** <u>**Ask of me, and I will make the nations your heritage, and the ends of the earth your possession**</u>**.** *You shall break them with a rod of iron and dash them in pieces like a potter's vessel." Now* **therefore, O kings, be wise; be warned, O rulers of the earth. Serve the LORD with fear, and rejoice with trembling. Kiss the Son, lest he be angry, and you perish in the way, for his wrath is quickly kindled. Blessed are all who take refuge in him.**
>
> ~ *Psalm 2 (emphasis added)*

As Dr. Greg Bahnsen so frequently queried by the light of this wondrous passage: **Do we really think that Jesus forgot to ask?**

Of course not.

And where does all of this lead?

To our mission: The Gospel-fueled Great Commission:

> *And Jesus came and said to them, "__All authority__ in heaven and __on earth has been given to me__. Go therefore and make disciples of __all__ nations, baptizing them in the name of the Father and of the Son and of the Holy Spirit, teaching them to observe __all that I have commanded__ you. And behold, I am with you always, to the end of the age."*
>
> ~ Matthew 28:18-20 (emphasis added)

So let's get to it…by His grace, for His glory, and to our eternal benefit.

So what do we do now?

With worship and open idolatry being such *giant* constructs that directly impact and define practically everything about a culture and civilization, **it is essential that we begin by repenting of our past and present embrace of any unbiblical approach to religious liberty**.

Repentance is the key.

It is the essential first step toward true restoration by the supernatural power of God and away from the increasing darkness into which our long running proud idolatry and rebellion has led (and continues to lead) us as a people.

There can be no excuses.

There can be no rationalizations.

There can be no justifications and no more "pro-America" spin.

There must be simple, clear repentance before God without any qualifications or defenses offered or imagined for what we have been actively celebrating as a virtue for many generations now: The open worship of false gods.

We have to stop coddling not only our sins (past and present), but the unbiblical works of men and women who have come before us. We cannot allow our appropriate appreciation of any man, group of men, or any man-made construct to be perverted into idolatry that makes them the "gold standard" for law or law-giver over and above the Word of God and God Himself, as we have been led to do by proponents of the religion of American Statism for many generations. We have to do this publicly and consistently. We have to incorporate this Spirit of true repentance into every area of our lives.

The sooner we bring *that* Spirit of personal humility and broken contriteness to the subjects of law, worship, education, economics, and everything else, the sooner we will be able to finally actively move to supernaturally restore those realms, all by God's grace, all for His glory, and all to our eternal benefit.

ACKNOWLEDGMENTS

First off, I must thank God (!) for the love, patience, endurance, encouragement and editing skills of my beautiful bride, Holly Mae. Her passion for the Word of God as the standard by which we might pursue, apply, and enjoy the beauty of God as revealed in every aspect of life is a matchless inspiration to me.

I'm also happily compelled to thank our church family at Christ the King Church in Middle Tennessee. Being led by God's grace into this local body of vibrant, supercool, and supernaturally encouraging Brothers and Sisters has been and continues to be a blessing on a scale that I can't really even begin to accurately convey here...but I do enjoy trying, so...

God has blessed Holly, Rosie, Wolfgang and me in many amazing ways through these beautiful Brothers and Sisters as we all struggle, fumble, strive and grow together by His grace and for His glory. The love of God's Nature as revealed in His Word is evident, inspiring, challenging and encouraging at Christ the King in ways that Holly and I had not previously experienced. We are very thankful to the Lord for connecting us with our dear Brothers and Sisters at Christ the King.

Many thanks also to Bojidar Marinov, Bill Evans, Joel McDurmon, Jeff Durbin, and the crew at Apologia Studios for all that they've done (and continue to do) for love of God's Nature as revealed in His Law and Word. The ongoing work of these folks continually moves and inspires us to know and love our Lord more on His terms, all by His grace, all for His glory, and all to our eternal benefit.

A great big shout out and thank you also goes to the many others who have connected with and supported the *Fire Breathing Christian* in these early days of its mission. Your regular daily pushback, feedback, encouragement, and (most importantly) prayers are more important than you may ever know in this side of eternity. Soli Deo gloria...and let's roll!

ABOUT THE AUTHOR

Photograph Copyright 2012 Cali Ashton Photography, Nashville, TN

Scott Alan Buss is a wretch saved by grace, a husband to Holly, and father to Rosie and Wolfgang. He and his family make their home in Middle Tennessee, where he is a thankful member of Christ the King Church.

Scott is a writer, speaker, and the founder of R3V Press, where he has published several books. He regularly blogs and podcasts at *Fire Breathing Christian*.

www.FireBreathingChristian.com

FIRE BREATHING

CHRISTIANS

This revised and updated edition of *Fire Breathing Christians* is 416 pages of Christ-centered, Gospel-fueled reformation, revival, and revolution.

ALSO FROM SCOTT ALAN BUSS AND R3VOLUTION PRESS:

The America Idol: How "We the People" Made the State Our God in Practice

On Education - Thoughts on Christ as the Essential Core of Children's Education

the beginning of knowledge - Christ as truth in apologetics

We Win Here - The Inevitable Triumph of the Gospel in Creation

Candy Christianity - America's Favorite Counterfeit Gospels

The American Child Sacrifice Machine

Fiat Slavery - The Economics of Hell (and America)

Fire Breathing Christians – The Common Believer's Call to Reformation, Revival, and Revolution

Apathetic Christianity: The Zombie Religion of American Churchianity

Satan's Jackass – The Progressive Party's War on Christianity

Stupid Elephant Tricks – The Other Progressive Party's War on Christianity

the

FIRE-BREATHING CHRISTIAN

PODCAST

HELL RAZING RADIO
www.FireBreathingChristian.com

For more *Stick People for Jesus* comics, visit
www.FireBreathingChristian.com.

Check out the latest Fire Breathing Tees designs
at www.FireBreathingChristian.com

HOME SCHOOL DESIGNS

ALL KNOW GOD DESIGNS

RAZE HELL DESIGNS

BE DANGEROUS DESIGNS

www.ingramcontent.com/pod-product-compliance
Lightning Source LLC
Chambersburg PA
CBHW051913170526
45168CB00001B/369